OPIUM

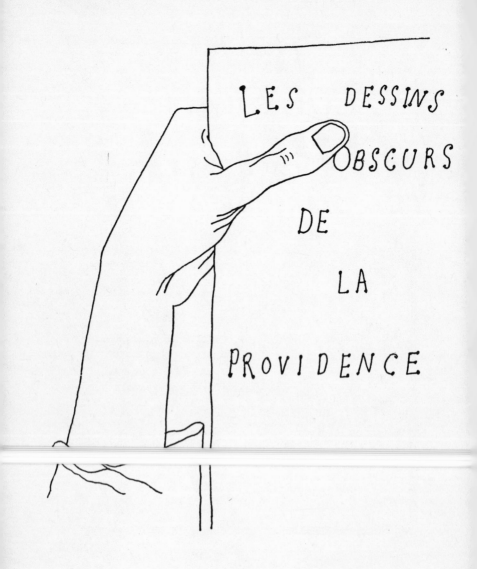

1   *The obscure designs of providence*

JEAN
COCTEAU
OPIUM
THE DIARY OF A CURE

GROVE PRESS, INC.   NEW YORK

Opium is published in three editions:
  An Evergreen Book (E-98)
  A hard bound edition
  A specially bound Limited Edition of 100 numbered copies

Grove Press Books and Evergreen Books
are published by Barney Rosset at Grove Press, Inc.
795 Broadway   New York 3, N. Y.

A New Translation
by
MARGARET CROSLAND
and
SINCLAIR ROAD
with
An Introduction
by the Translators
and the complete set of forty
three Original Drawings made
for the First French edition
by
THE AUTHOR

DEDICATED TO JEAN DESBORDES

There are spots even on the sun. There are none on your heart. Each day you grant me this spectacle: your surprise at learning of the existence of evil.

You have just written *Les Tragédiens*, a book above all syntax. As an epigraph you quote four lines of my poetry. I offer you these notes in exchange, for you possess naturally this 'profound lightness' which opium imitates to a small extent.

Mon cher bon grand fond malempia.

La Séquestrée de Poitiers
(From the study by André Gide)

CONTENTS

ILLUSTRATIONS
BY JEAN COCTEAU

Introduction

by the Translators

Living in the twentieth century is so intolerably dull or exasperating for so many people that a great number of them, in the hope of creating escape, excitement or rest, force their body and soul into a monstrous union by taking drugs. Even greater numbers of people who lack the courage to take them enjoy reading books about those who do. Cocteau's contribution to this curious branch of literature is unique. His *Opium,* The Journal of a Cure, is a set of notes written in 1929 with substantial additions made to the proofs the following year. It evokes the night and day of the opium world in a style of its own, through drawings that are tranquil or agonised, and through writing them is "sensational" only in the original meaning of the word, by which unnatural states are transmuted into an ashen poetry, until even the smoke that rises from the cabins of the Saïgon boat turns into the grey clouds of distant olive trees.

Cocteau's *Opium* is of course about Cocteau, and only incidentally does it describe the delights of the addicted and the miseries of the cured. About opium itself Cocteau does not discover a great deal that is new, either from a scientific or a personal angle. Many of his remarks naturally appear paradoxical and unexpected, even if Thomas De Quincey, writing a hundred years earlier, had in several cases reached the same conclusions. Cocteau's methods form an interesting contrast to those of his predecessor, who wrote several pages proving that the effects of alcohol were quite different from the effects of opium. Cocteau came to the same conclusion, but he wrote only two sentences.

The value of Cocteau's remarks about opium lies obviously in the way he makes them, in that sad and splendid aphoristic turn of phrase that marks everything he writes. In one sense Cocteau lost the battle with opium; he could not give himself to it entirely, the cost was too great. The plea in this book that medicine should learn to make opium harmless rather than deal passively with its after-effects is that of an intelligent person. It is not original, and here again De Quincey in his rambling way had made the same suggestion in his book. But Cocteau's description of the actual cure, the stages in being 'weaned,' as he says, from the milk of Paradise, has an undeniable value. This aspect of the journal contributes something that cannot be found in any medical treatise or in any of those flat, dull books whose authors try to

drugs.

Opium is not easy reading, for it was not easy writing. If Cocteau had merely been making descriptive notes of how he felt from day to day it would still have required a considerable effort to write them; but along with physical change he was attempting to describe what can only be called spiritual adaptation. Elusive, subtle, changing from hour to hour, his thoughts and feelings needed clarifying, and this could only be done by writing them down. Many writers would have left only disembodied jottings which might have been a useful record but nothing more. Cocteau's journal is often staccato, obscure and without any apparent continuity. And yet, because it is written by Cocteau, it has the deeply-hidden but satisfying unity of a strange poetry. After two or three readings its themes, expressed in different keys, and played at varying speeds, emerge in the simplicity of their original conception, while the orchestral *bravura* dies away.

There are other reasons why this Journal of a Cure, collection of notes though it is, occupies a place of its own in Cocteau's world. He regards *La Difficulté d'Etre* as the key to his house, yet *Opium* could be a useful guide-book. It stands on its own, at least as far as any of the autobiographical *poésie critique* does so, but amongst its own leaves lie tendrils which have grown across from other plants. It illustrates the vital interdependence of Cocteau's work and the degree to which one's enjoyment of his writing is increased and illuminated by knowing it thoroughly. In *Opium* he looks forward and backward, and we see just how closely he identifies himself with his work. There is the fascinating description of how *Les Enfants Terribles* (*Children of the Game*) came into being, how Jacques Chardonne urged him to write a full-length work, how the end of the book came into his head first, how a poem and a tune stimulated him. The novel was published just before these notes were written, and on page 144 Cocteau says 'My next work will be a film.' *Le Sang d'un Poète*, first shown in 1932, contains a mysterious but poetic version of the snowballing episode which is such an integral part of *Les Enfants Terribles*. Then, in 1950 Cocteau created the wonderful film based on the novel itself. Going back once more, but forward in time from *Opium*, Chapter VIII of *Portraits-Souvenir* (VII in *Paris Album*) describes the Cité Monthiers, Dargelos and the snowball fight once again. Thus a scene and an incident which occupy a central place in Cocteau's mythology appear in a novel, two films and at least two sections of the *poésie critique*, including *Opium*.

Sometimes Cocteau forgets how much his readers are likely to know. The reference to the 'purge scene' on page 104 for instance is made comprehensible only with a knowledge of that amusing chapter in *Portraits-Souvenir* which tells the whole story. The same may be said of the many references to the poems in *Opéra* and the puns (for example the two ~~meanings of the verb *voler*~~) which have never been popular with his admirers in spite of ~~his own~~ attempts to justify them. *L'ami Zamore de Madame Du-Barry* takes on a new significance—even if it does not impress us—when we know that it occurs elsewhere as *La mise à mort de Madame Dubarry*.

Cocteau's detractors have often remarked that the interdependence of his work is nothing more than an absence of self-discipline, a paucity of ideas and a tedious, interminable attempt to justify himself. This criticism is meaningless, for Cocteau's discipline is exercised in another realm. Justify himself he does, remaining strangely patient before a dense and unsympathetic public. Something of his supposed and his genuine attitude can be understood from the pages about *La Voix Humaine,* which was successfully produced at the Comédie Française while *Opium* was being written. In fairness to Cocteau it must be admitted that he works just as hard to explain his successes as his failures, although from his point of view this arbitrary division into black and white does not exist.

There is every chance that Cocteau, like other members of his family, would have been successful at the bar, provided that he could always have been counsel for the defence; and *Opium,* like so many others of his books, embodies several pages of impressive apologia. Few writers of any age have been such persuasive propagandists for those of their contemporaries whom they believed to be important. When Cocteau admires a writer or an artist, an actor or a circus clown he is not concerned with critical analysis; his admiration is whole-hearted or it does not exist at all. The dedication of *Opium* to Jean Desbordes is typical in its unqualified eulogy. But how many people outside France (or even within) have heard of him? How many have read *J'Adore, Les Tragédiens* or even *Le Vrai Visage du Marquis de Sade,* fascinating study though it is? Cocteau's belief that Desbordes was a writer of great value may even have been justified if his young friend had not lost his life in the war of 1939—45.

Raymond Roussel the surrealist, Inaudi the calculator, Eisenstein and Bunuel the film directors—a strange gallery of figures whose reputations have met varying fates as time passes. Their counterparts in other books are Edouard de Max, the actor, Barbette the acrobat, Chirico the painter. There is no more solitary figure than Cocteau, but no one with a greater genius for friendship and admiration.

The pages about Roussel illuminate his work; the pages about Proust on the other hand illuminate the man. A great deal has been written in an attempt to explain every aspect of his writing and living; but perhaps in the end it is Proust among the dust sheets, 'like Carnot dead,' who remains in the memory. Nobody can rival Cocteau in *portraits-souvenir* of this type; they are portraits that only a poet can draw.

Since *Opium* is a microcosm of Cocteau, nearly all his favourite themes recur there, like a whole row of King Charles' heads. They range from the role of the poet as a seer, and the necessity for remaining in the deep creative sleep of poetry to the fact that 'Victor Hugo was a madman who believed himself to be Victor Hugo,' or the problems of realism in the theatre. The Cocteau-enthusiast will be delighted to hear so many favourite stories again and to recognise that unmistakable voice saying quite seriously, 'I detest originality. I avoid it as much as possible.'

Opium could perhaps be recommended as an introduction to Cocteau's work in the sense that it appears to be about something, about opium. One can enjoy it without wishing to learn anything about that time-honoured nepenthe. If one already knows something about it then Cocteau adds his usual paradoxical illumination, his poet's interpretation. If one knows nothing about opium one will learn only a little. If one knows nothing about Cocteau, then one will want to know and read a great deal more.

M. C.
S. R.

Opium

These drawings and notes date from the clinic in St. Cloud (December 16th 1928 to April 1929).[1]

They are addressed to the opium addicts, the victims, the unknown friends enlisted by books, the sole excuse for writing them.

I have omitted the drawings I did under the pretext of distracting myself. Whether I like it or not, they reveal my preoccupation with form, however great my stupidity in the face of the daily problems I had to meet. I am describing a cure: a wound in slow motion. The drawings which follow are cries of pain in slow motion, and the notes are the stages in passing from a state considered as abnormal to a state considered as normal.

Here the Public Prosecutor rises. But I do not give evidence. I do not plead. I do not pass judgment. I merely produce documents, for and against, in the

I shall undoubtedly be accused of a lack of manners. I would like to lack manners. It is difficult. Lack of manners is the sign of a hero.[2]

I am speaking of a lack of manners made up of figures, hotel bills and soiled linen.

[1] The notes dated 1930 were added at the proof stage.
[2] The mark of a military hero is disobedience, the lack of discipline.

2 *Drawing*

3   *Exquisite pain*

The leitmotiv of DE PROFUNDIS.[1]

The only crime is to be superficial. Everything which is understood is good.

The repetition of this sentence is irritating but revealing. This commonplace, Wilde's last discovery, ceases to be a commonplace and begins to live by the mere fact of his discovering it. It acquires the importance of a date.

I would rather not be concerned any more about writing well or badly; and achieve the style of numbers.

I would like to know if Wilde's letter is as slapdash as its translation. That would be a victory over aesthetics.

One turns from this letter with the impression of having read a masterpiece of style, because everything in it is true. Everything in it has that dead weight of circumstantial detail which is essential for establishing an alibi, essential for ruining or saving a man.

Rousseau decorates his numbers. He curls them, writes them with a flourish. Chopin puts garlands round his. Their times demanded it. But they both lacked manners. They washed their dirty linen *en famille,* that is in public, among the family which they seek and find for themselves. They bleed ink. They are heroes.

*   *   *

I became addicted to opium a second time under the following circumstances.

[1] Oscar Wilde's letter to Lord Alfred Douglas.

To begin with, I could not have been thoroughly cured the first time. Many courageous drug addicts do not know the pitfalls of being cured, they are content merely to give up and emerge ravaged by a useless ordeal, their cells weakened and further prevented from regaining their vitality through alcohol and sport.

Incredible phenomena are attached to the cure; medicine is powerless against them, beyond making the padded cell look like a hotel-room and demanding of the doctor or nurse patience, attendance and sensitivity. I shall explain later that these phenomena should be not those of an organism in a state of decomposition but on the contrary the uncommunicated symptoms of a baby at the breast and of vegetables in spring.

A tree must suffer from the rising of its sap and not feel the falling of its leaves.

"Le Sacre Du Printemps" orchestrates a cure with a scrupulous precision of which Stravinsky is not even aware.

I therefore became an opium addict again because the doctors who cure—one should really say, quite simply, who purge—do not seek to cure the troubles

my unbalanced state of mind; and I preferred an artificial equilibrium to no equilibrium at all. This moral disguise is more misleading than a disordered appearance: it is human, almost feminine, to have recourse to it.

I became addicted with caution and under medical

supervision. There *are* doctors capable of pity. I never exceeded ten pipes. I smoked them at the rate of three in the morning (at nine o'clock), four in the afternoon (at five o'clock), three in the evening (at eleven o'clock). I believed that, in this way, I was reducing the chances of addiction. With opium I suckled new cells, which were restored to the world after five months of abstinence, and I suckled them with countless unknown alkaloids, whereas a morphine addict, whose habits frighten me, fills his veins with a single known poison and surrenders himself far less to the unknown.

*   *   *

I am writing these lines after twelve days and twelve nights without sleep. I leave to the drawings the task of expressing the tortures inflicted by medical impotence on those who drive out a remedy which is in process of becoming a despot.

*   *   *

A morphine addict's blood shows no trace of morphine. It is tempting to imagine the day when doctors will discover the hiding places of morphine and will lure it out by using some substance to which it is partial, like a snake with a bowl of milk. But it will still be necessary for the organism to withstand the abrupt transition from an autumn to a spring.

Until this discovery is made, science risks making mistakes, just as hypnosis was used for hysterics before the experiments of Dr. Sollier, experiments which consist in treating hysteria as a pathological sleep and in waking the patient gradually, instead of adding evil to evil by a method which used to amount to treating a morphine addict with morphine.

*   *   *

I believe that nature inflicts on us the code of Sparta and the termite colony. Should we circumvent it? Where do our prerogatives stop? Where does the forbidden zone begin?

*   *   *

Opium leads the organism towards death in euphoric mood. The tortures arise from the process of returning to life against one's wish. A whole spring-time excites the veins to madness, bringing with it ice and fiery lava.

I recommend the patient who has been deprived for eight days to bury his head in his arm, to glue his ear to that arm, and wait. Catastrophe, riots, factories blowing up, armies in flight, detect a whole apocalypse in the starry night of the human body.

*   *   *

Milk, the antidote to morphine. A friend of mine

detests milk. When she was injected with morphine after an operation, she asked for milk and liked it. The following day she could no longer take it.

*　　　*　　　*

A person undergoing a cure experiences brief periods of sleep, and awakenings which remove the taste for sleep. The organism seems to emerge from hibernation, that strange economy of tortoises, marmots and crocodiles. Our blindness, our obstinacy in judging everything according to our own rhythm of existence, used to lead us to mistake the slowness of plant life for an absurd serenity. Nothing illustrates better the drama of a cure than those speeded-up films which expose the grimaces, gestures and contortions of the vegetable kingdom. The same progress in the world of sound will no doubt enable us to hear the cries of plants.

*　　　*　　　*

Progress. Is it a good thing to give birth in the American fashion, with anaesthetics and forceps? And is not this kind of progress, which consists in suffering less, a symptom, like the machine, of a universe in which exhausted mankind substitutes other forces for its own, avoiding shocks to a weakened nervous system?

*　　　*　　　*

There is still no such thing as a scientific cure. No sooner are the alkaloids in the blood, than they fix upon certain tissues. Morphine becomes a phantom, a shadow, a fairy. One can imagine how the known and unknown opium alkaloids work, their Chinese invasion. To overcome them, one must have recourse to the methods of Molière. One drains the patient, cleans him out, stirs up his bile and, whether one likes it or not, goes back to those tales according to which evil spirits were supposed to be chased out by herbs, charms, purges and emetics.

*   *   *

Do not expect me to be a traitor. Of course opium remains unique and the euphoria it induces superior to that of health. I owe it my perfect hours. It is a pity that instead of perfecting curative techniques, medicine does not try to render opium harmless.

But here we come back to the problem of progress. Is suffering a regulation or a lyrical interlude?

It seems to me that on an earth so old, so wrinkled, so painted, where so many compromises and laughable conventions are rife, opium (if its harmful effects could be eliminated) would and would cause more good than the fever of activity causes harm.

My nurse says to me "You are the first patient whom I have seen writing on the eighth day."

I fully realise that I am planting a spoon in the soft tapioca of my young cells, that I am delaying matters, but I am burning myself up and will always do so. In two weeks, despite these notes, I shall no longer believe in what I am experiencing now. One must leave behind a trace of this journey which memory forgets. One must, when this is impossible, write or draw without responding to the romantic solicitations of pain, without enjoying suffering like music, tieing a pen to one's foot if need be, helping the doctors who can learn nothing from laziness.

During an attack of neuritis one night, I asked B.: "You, who do not practise and are up to your eyes in work at the Salpêtrière and are preparing your thesis, why do you attend me at my home day and night? I know doctors. You like me very much but you like medicine more." He replied that he had at last found a patient who talked, that he learnt more from me, because I was capable of describing my symptoms, than at the Salpêtrière where the question: "Where does it hurt?" invariably brought the same reply: "Don't know, doctor."

*   *   *

The reawakening of one's senses (the first clear symptom of recovery) is accompanied by sneezes, yawns, sniffling and tears. Another sign: the poultry in the hen house opposite exasperated me and so did those pigeons which trot up and down the tin roof, their hands behind their backs. On the seventh day the crow of the cock pleased me. I am writing these notes between six and seven in the morning. With opium nothing exists before eleven o'clock.

*　　　　　*　　　　　*

Clinics receive few opium addicts. It is rare for an opium addict to stop smoking. The nurses only know the counterfeit smokers, the elegant smokers, those who combine opium, alcohol, drugs, the setting (opium and alcohol are mortal enemies), or those who pass from the pipe to the syringe and from morphine to heroin. Of all drugs "the drug" is the most subtle. The lungs absorb its smoke instantaneously. The effect of a pipe is immediate. I am speaking of the real smokers. The amateurs feel nothing, they wait for dreams and risk being seasick; because the effectiveness of opium is the result of a pact. If we fall under its spell, we shall never be able to give it up.

To moralise to an opium addict is like saying to Tristan: "Kill Yseult. You will feel much better afterwards."

*　　　　　*　　　　　*

Opium .... has impatient addicts, bunglers. It moves away, leaving them morphine, heroin, suicide and death.

*　　　　　*　　　　　*

If you hear someone say: "X . . . has killed himself smoking opium," you should know that it is

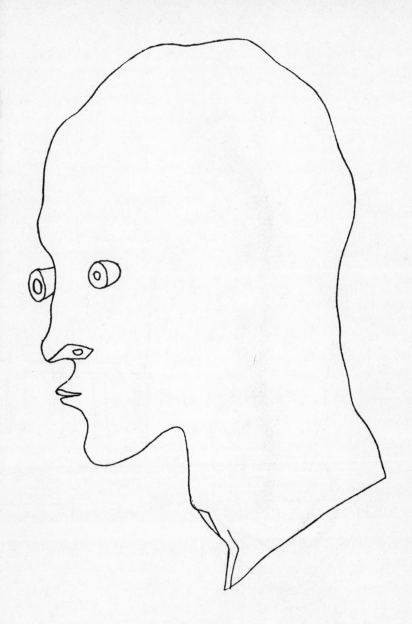

4   *Bird*

5 *Drawing*

6 Drawing

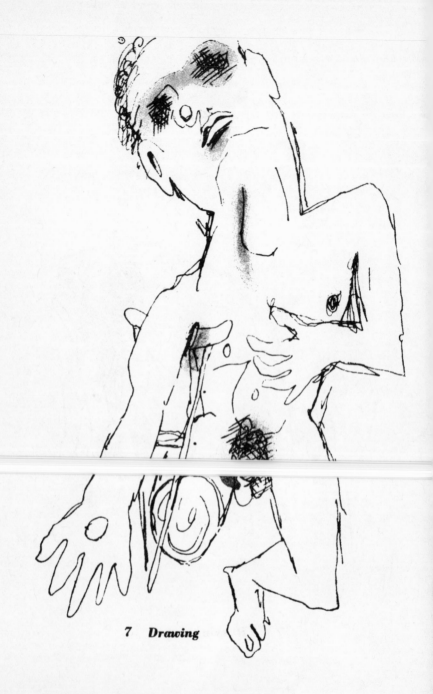

7   *Drawing*

impossible, and that this death conceals something else.

*   *   *

Certain organisms are born to become a prey to drugs. They demand a corrective, without which they can have no contact with the outside world. They float. They vegetate in the half-light. The world remains unreal, until some substance has given it body.

It does happen that these unfortunates can live without ever finding the slightest remedy. It does happen, too, that the remedy they find kills them.

It is a matter of luck when opium steadies them and provides these souls of cork with a diver's suit. For the harm done by opium will be less than that caused by other substances and less than the infirmity which they try to heal.

*   *   *

When I speak of young cells, I am not speaking of nerve cells which are created once and for all and never change.

*   *   *

With a man, the awakening process of weaning manifests itself physiologically, but with a woman the symptoms are mainly psychological. With a man

27

the drug does not put his heart to sleep, but his sexuality. With a woman it arouses her sexuality and puts her heart to sleep. On the eighteenth day of weaning a woman becomes tender and whimpers. That is why, in clinics for drug addicts, the female patients all appear to be in love with the doctor.

*   *   *

Tobacco is almost harmless. After combustion, the nicotine disappears. It is customary to confuse nicotine, which is a white powder, with the kind of yellow paste produced by the pyrotechnical change in the combustible materials. It would take four or five big cigars a day to produce a heart-attack. Most of the notorious ravages of tobacco are spasmodic phenomena without real danger. They are exaggerated, as Michelet wondrously exaggerates the role of coffee.

*   *   *

Young Asia no longer smokes because "grandfather
father did not smoke." Since, alas, young Asia imitates young Europe, it is through us that opium will return to its starting point.

*   *   *

A letter from H . . . , who gave up opium on his

own with unheard-of courage. I knew the effort was useless, I knew the confusion between giving up oneself and giving up the drug, and I expected pessimistic news after the first optimistic letters.

1. Too much exercise; 2. Recourse to alcohol (the letters just before the last); 3. (the last letter) The break-down. "I feel ill—how am I to describe it to you?—in my 'great divide.'" Do you recognise the great sympathetic nervous system, the terrible mountain chain of nerves, the armature of the soul?

If the organism rejects the drug, this is its last refuge. Drive opium off the ship, and it hides in the engine-room.

*　　　*　　　*

A car can massage organs which no masseur can reach. It is the only remedy for the disorders of the great sympathetic nervous system. The craving for opium can be endured in a car.

Clinics for addicts should have attached to them, in the first place, a medical masseur and electrical massage equipment. With hydrotherapy it is not the water from the shower which calms, but the spray. Baths can be upsetting, they drove me mad.

*　　　*　　　*

I remain convinced, despite my failures, that opium can be good and that it is entirely up to us to make it well-disposed. We must know how to handle it. Nothing is worse than clumsiness on our part. A strict regime (laxatives, exercise, perspiration, rest-periods, care of the liver, keeping hours which do not encroach on one's night sleep) would permit the use of a remedy jeopardised by half-wits.

Let no one say to me: "Habit forces the smoker to increase the dose." One of the riddles of opium is that the smoker never has to increase his dose.

*　　　　　*　　　　　*

The drama of opium, as I see it, is none other than the drama of comfort and the lack of comfort. Comfort kills. Lack of comfort creates. I am speaking of the lack of both material and spiritual comfort.

To take opium without yielding to the absolute comfort which it offers is to escape, within the domain of the spirit, from the stupid worries of life which have nothing to do with the lack of comfort in the domain of the senses.

*　　　　　*　　　　　*

If a hermit lives in a state of ecstasy, his lack of comfort becomes luxury. He must relinquish it.

*　　　　　*　　　　　*

There is in man a sort of fixative, that is to say, a sort of absurd feeling stronger than reason which allows him to think that the children who play are a race of dwarfs, instead of being a bunch of "get out of there and leave room for me."

Living is a horizontal fall.

Without this fixative any life perfectly and continually conscious of its speed would become intolerable. It enables the condemned man to sleep.

I lack this fixative. It is, I suppose, a diseased gland. Medicine takes this infirmity for an excess of conscience, for an intellectual advantage.

Everything convinces me of the functioning, in others, of this absurd fixative, as indispensable as habit, which conceals from us each day the horror of having to get up, shave, dress and eat. Even if it were only the photograph album, one of the most comical ways of turning a helter-skelter into a succession of solemn monuments.

Opium gave me this fixative. Without opium, plans, marriages and journeys appear to me just as foolish as if someone falling out of a window were to hope to make friends with the occupants of the room before which he passes.

* * *

If the universe were not moved by a very simple mechanism, it would break down. The whole of this movement, which seems to us a complicated timepiece, must resemble an alarm-clock. Thus the need to procreate is doled out to us by the gross, blindly. A mistake does not cost nature much, given the odds in her favour. A mistake which becomes refined, a vice, is nothing more than one of nature's luxuries.

*   *   *

THE PLACE OF MALLARME

Youth, enamoured of the marvellous and the cynical, prefers any fair-ground clairvoyant, any crook, to this type of gentleman, upright bourgeois, exquisite aristocrat, devoted worker, goldsmith— Mallarmé. Human, too human. For my part, once the shadow which rings him like a halo has disappeared, I admit to seeing no more than "modern style" jewellery.

If Mallarmé cuts stones, it is not so much diamond as amethyst, opal, or a gem from Herodias' tiara in the Gustave Moreau museum.

Rimbaud stole his diamonds; but where from? That is the riddle.

Mallarmé, the scholar, bores us. He deserves that dubious dedication to *Les Fleurs du Mal* which Gautier does not deserve. Rimbaud retains the aura of a receiver, the aura of blood, he cuts diamonds for the purpose of breaking-in, for the sole end of cutting

The real leaders of youth between 1912 and 1930 were Rimbaud, Ducasse, Nerval and Sade.

Mallarmé influences rather the style of journalism.

Baudelaire becomes wrinkled, but preserves an astonishing youthfulness.

Each verse of Mallarmé was, from birth, a beautiful wrinkle, delicate, studious, noble, profound. This air of being older than the eternal prevents his work from growing old in places, and gives it instead an overall appearance of being wrinkled, like the lines in a hand, lines which should be decorative instead of prophetic.

*   *   *

Nothing is more sad than Jules Renard's journal, nothing reveals more clearly the awfulness of "letters." He must have said to himself: "Everyone is mean, small, unscrupulously ambitious. No one dares admit it; I shall admit it and I shall be unique." The result, in the case of the respectable reader who enjoys Renard, is an unsurmountable sense of embarrassment.

One leaves this breviary of the man of letters, this philosophy of scrupulously unscrupulous ambition, with the certainty that the frogs have found a king. (By frogs I mean anything that is caught with a piece of red ribbon).

A little insecticide would destroy those volumes which make us itch, and prevent us from re-reading POIL DE CAROTTE.

*   *   *

I suppose that many journalists do not want to lie but lie they do, in the effort to obtain style, by using the mechanism of poetry and history, which gradu-

33

ally distorts. This distortion, applied directly, has the effect of a lie. Now I do not know if this lie, to which facts eventually owe their prominence, is useful without perspective. I believe that facts, faithfully reported when they are still fresh the following morning, would have a thousand times more force.

* * *

MARVELS

Tarquinius Superbus decapitates poppies (the very symbol of activity), Jesus blasts an innocent tree, Lenin sows the earth with bricks; Saint-Just, the delightful throat-slitter with the slit throat; and young Russian girls of the revolution whose breasts were bombs; and the forbidden, fabulous opium.

* * *

The purity of a revolution can last a fortnight.

That is why a poet, the revolutionary of the soul, limits himself to the about-turns of the mind.

Every fortnight I change my programme. For me opium is a revolt. Addiction a revolt. The cure a revolt. I do not talk of my works. Each one guillotines

* * *

Phaedra, or organic faithfulness. Legally one must be faithful to one person, humanly to a type. Phaedra is faithful to a type. Hers is not an example of love,

8   Drawing

9   Fear giving wings to courage

but the example of love itself. And then, where is the incest? Hippolytus is not her son. It is proper that Phaedra should respect Theseus and that Theseus should love Hippolytus. It is human that Phaedra should love Hippolytus and that Theseus should detest him.

*   *   *

We are no longer, alas, a race of farmers and shepherds. The fact that we need another system of therapy to defend our over-worked nervous system cannot be questioned. For that reason it is imperative to discover some means of rendering harmless those beneficial substances which the body eliminates so unsatisfactorily, or of shielding the nerve cells.

*   *   *

Tell this obvious truth to a doctor and he will shrug his shoulders. He talks of literature, Utopia, and the obsessions of the drug addict.

Nevertheless, I contend that one day we shall use those soothing substances without danger, that we shall avoid habit-making, that we shall laugh at the bugaboo of the drug and that opium, once tamed, will assuage the evil of towns where trees die on their feet.

*   *   *

The mortal boredom of the smoker who is cured!

Everything one does in life, even love, occurs in an express train racing towards death. To smoke opium is to get out of the train while it is still moving. It is to concern oneself with something other than life, with death.

*   *   *

If a smoker, damaged by the drug, questions himself sincerely, he will always find some fault for which he is paying and it turns opium against him.

*   *   *

The patience of a poppy. He who has smoked will smoke. Opium knows how to wait.

*   *   *

Opium chastens one's ambitions.

*   *   *

(the time of LE CAP[1]) being filled with anguish at certain images. I said to myself, for example: "I am going to die and I shall not have conveyed the swallows' cries," or "I shall die without having explained the setting of empty cities at night." The Seine, the posters, tar in April, the river steamers—I took no

[1] *Le Cap de Bonne Esperance*, poems published in 1919. (Tr.)

pleasure in all these wonders. I only experienced the anguish of living too short a time to tell of them.

Having told these things, I experienced a great sense of relief. I observed with detachment. After the war the things that I hoped to say were of an increasingly uncommon kind, limited to a very few. No one could take them from me or anticipate me. I drew breath like a runner who turns round, lies down, recovers his composure and does not even see the silhouettes of the others on the horizon any more.

*　　　*　　　*

This evening I very much want to re-read the *Sketches of Malte Laurids Brigge*, but I do not want to ask for books, I want to read what happens to drop into this room.

If only the *Sketches* were to be found among the books the patients left for the nurses! No. M . . . has only got Paul Féval, and Féval the Younger. I have already exhausted the families of d'Artagnan and Lagardère. In the Rue d'Anjou they got me the copy from Emile-Paul.

I would read again about the death of Christoph Detlev Brigge or the death of the Téméraire. I would see again the corner room in Rodin's house, the Hôtel Biron, in 1912, and the lamp of his German secretary, Mr. Rilke. I lived in the former building of the Sisters of the Sacred Heart, which is now destroyed. My French windows opened on to seventeen acres of abandoned garden which runs along the Boulevard des Invalides. I knew nothing of Mr. Rilke. I knew nothing of anything. I was terribly alert, ambitious, absurd. I needed sleep to understand, to live and to regret. Much later, in 1916, Cendrars revealed Rilke to me, and much later still, in 1921, Mme K . . . sent me the bewildering telegram: *"Tell Cocteau that I adore him, the only person for whom myth opens its gates and from where he returns bronzed as from the seaside."*

That was about *Orphée,* from the man who wrote: *We had a different conception of the marvellous. We found that, when everything happened naturally, things were even more strange.*

And to say after these very lofty rewards that one is sometimes irritated by an article!

How vulnerable we are, once awakened from those sleeps of which death is the apotheosis, those sleeps between which one should always remain quiet, awaiting their return, instead of wanting to be important and joining in the conversation of the grownups and saying one's piece, and saying it in such a way that one would pay dearly afterwards for having been silent.

written while awake, except the books which preceded *Le Potomak*,[1] when I began to go to sleep: but I have some. How much would I give not to have them exist.

*   *   *

[1] First Published in 1919, although written a few years earlier. (Tr.)

I noticed, when playing Heurtebise in *Orphée,* that the most attentive audience exchanges remarks; that it misses therefore some essential scrap of dialogue.

Does the theatre demand that one should be slap-dash? Are the padding, the slow changes of scene inevitable? Cannot one force the audience to be quiet?

Through Talma, Hugo condemns pompous verse in the theatre. In fact, it is impossible for rhymes like *âme* and *femme* to occur every dozen lines in Hugo's plays without his being intentionally slap-dash. That is the way in which Victor Hugo, otherwise very painstaking, approaches the beauties of *Fantomas.*

Notre Dame de Paris, and *L'Homme Qui Rit* are romanticised melodramas. Hugo despises the theatre. In it he finds a vehicle. Is it a system or just careless-ness? A system, because Hugo's dramas can still fill the house, like Wagner's.

One asks oneself whether the audience could not, in the long run, become attentive. Through having been prepared and hypnotised, by having had rhymes tossed to it like bones to keep its nostrils twitching, the audience has been corrupted. It is not that I advise against rhyme in itself, but against that artful sound whose sole purpose is to prevent the audience from falling asleep.

*   *   *

When I was completely under the spell of opium, I used to sleep interminable sleeps lasting half a second. One day, when I went to see Picasso in the Rue La Boétie, I thought in the lift that I was growing taller side by side with something indefinably terrible which would last for ever. A voice cried out: "My name can be found on the plate." A jolt awakened me and I read on the brass plate: HEURTE-BISE. I recall that at Picasso's we talked about miracles; Picasso said that everything was a miracle, and it was a miracle that one did not dissolve in one's bath like a lump of sugar. A little while afterwards the angel Heurtebise haunted me and I began the poem. On my next visit I looked at the plate. It bore the name OTIS-PIFRE; the lift had changed its make.

I finished *L'Ange Heurtebise,* a poem inspired and formal at the same time like chess, on the eve of my cure, in the rue de Chateaubriand. (The Thermes Clinic has been destroyed: the first pick-axe blow fell on the day of my departure). Afterwards I called the angel in *Orphée,* Heurtebise. I quote the origin of the name because of the countless coincidences which it still causes.

Since Marcel Herrand wished to rehearse the play the night before it opened, we met in my flat in the rue d'Anjou. We rehearsed in the hall and Herrand had just said: *"With these gloves you will pass through mirrors as through water,"* when a frightful noise was heard inside the flat. Of a tall mirror in the washroom only the frame remained. The glass, shattered, was strewn on the ground.

Glenway Westcott and Monroe Wheeler, who had come to Paris for the première of *Orphée,* were held up on the way to the theatre by a collision in the boulevard Raspail; a window was broken and a white horse stuck its head into the cab.

One year later I was lunching with them in Villefranche-sur-Mer, where they were sharing a very isolated house on the hill. They were translating *Orphée* and told me how incomprehensible a glazier would be in America. I countered by quoting "The Kid" in which Chaplin plays the part of a glazier in New York. "It is rare in New York and rare in Paris," I said to them, "one hardly ever meets one." They asked me to describe a glazier and were escorting me across the garden to the gate, when we heard and saw a glazier who, against all expectation and probability, passed along the empty road and disappeared.

Orphée was being played in Spanish in Mexico. An earthquake interrupted the scene of the bacchantes, demolished the theatre and injured several people. When the theatre was rebuilt, *Orphée* was given again. Suddenly, a stage manager announced that the play could not continue. The actor playing the part of Orphée, before re-emerging from the mirror, had fallen dead in the wings.

The Vicomte and Vicomtesse Charles de Noailles had hidden the children's Easter eggs in the sand in a gymnasium on their estate in the South of France. They asked a young mason, who was working in the

garden, and whom they called Heurtebise because of
his white silhouette, to hang up some paper chains
above some sand. The young man climbed up on to
the glass roof, slipped through it and fell, without
doing himself any harm, flat on his stomach in the
sand, his back covered with broken panes. On being
questioned, the young man said his name was Ange.

The Princesse E. de Polignac bought a house in
the country and asked the young under-gardener his
name: Raphaël Heurtebise.[1]

*　　　*　　　*

Trusting and credulous as I am, it is normal for
me to be continually on my guard and not to read a
supernatural significance into events too quickly. One
must never get excited about mystery, so that mystery
may come on its own and not find the path confused
by our impatience to make contact with it.

Don't forget that official contacts with the unknown
always finish in some commercialised undertaking
like Lourdes, or in a police raid, like Gilles de Rais.

It is revolting to deny it.

But whether we cheat, deliberately or without
knowing it, by interposing some force which is
released by our impatience, it comes to the same

[1] Since the marvellous originates in an order which gets slightly out of
gear, it is understandable that it should always manifest itself to us
on points of no importance. This causes it to be confused with minor
coincidences.

10 Drawing

11   Drawing

12 *Scene from Orphée*

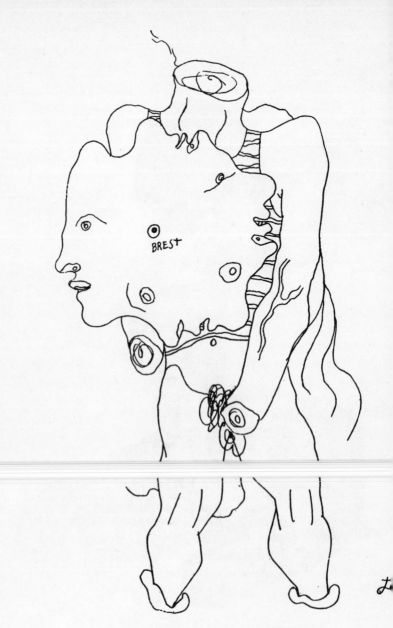

13 Question of manners

thing as far as contact with the unknown is concerned.

The more eager we are, the more indispensable it is to push back, at whatever cost, the frontiers of the marvellous.

We talk a great deal about greatness and mystery. Rarely do we prove their existence. A fine lesson in greatness and mystery—the Bénévol-Robertson-Inaudi—Madame Lucile show at the Ambigu. These unsophisticated artists work honestly and directly, face to face with the unknown. The eyes of Madame Lucile, the haughtiness of Bénévol, the authority and the charm of Inaudi. Inaudi is the same type as Berthelot and Bergson. No vulgarity. The unworthy hall calls out the figures 606, 69. He never takes any notice. His graciousness, when he crushes a pretentious accountant or a lady who mistakes the date. His tiny fingers darting to and fro. The whole thing finishes by being like beauty itself. Under that avalanche of figures, which I do not understand at all, I used to have tears in my eyes and my heart would beat to the point of bursting.

The Davenport brothers' cupboard, Bénévol's trunk, so many works of art which throw light on Poe's study of the chess player. But what kind of study should one write? A miracle ceases to be a miracle by the mere fact of happening. There the miracle lives on. The trick does not deceive. And when a trick reaches the simplicity of no longer being a trick, I mean when Bénévol hypnotises, when Madame Lucile divines, this show, from which the mere dilettante of the circus, the music-hall, the brothel or the fair will get nothing, this show without showmanship, these artists without art, these exquisite giants reminded me of a box at the Ballet Russe, where one evening we saw Picasso, Matisse, Derain and Braque together, and of that sublime woman's cry (reported by Barrès) at the burial of Verlaine: "Verlaine! All your friends are here."

*   *   *

(1930) Those small hotel rooms in which I have camped for so many years, rooms to make love in, but where I make friends unceasingly, an occupation a thousand times more exhausting than making love.

On leaving Saint-Cloud, I repeated to myself: it is April. I am strong. I have a book which I did not expect. Any room in any hotel will be good. But my death-like room in the rue Bonaparte became a room for death. I had forgotten that opium transfigures the world and that, without opium, a sinister room remains a sinister room.

One of the wonders of opium is to transform instantaneously an unknown room into a room so familiar, so full of memories, that one thinks one has always occupied it. When addicts go away they suffer no hurt because of the certainty that the delicate mechanism will function in one minute, anywhere.

After five pipes an idea would become distorted, diffused slowly in the water of the body with all the noble whims of Chinese ink, fore-shortened like a black diver.

*   *   *

A dressing-gown in holes, stained and burnt by cigarettes, gives the addict away.

An extraordinary photograph in a sensational magazine: the beheading of a Chinese rebel. The execution and the sword are still blurred like an electric fan as it stops. A spray of blood shoots out of the trunk, quite straight. The head, smiling, has fallen on to the rebel's knees, like the smoker's cigarette, without his noticing it.

He will notice it tomorrow by the blood stain, like the addict by the burn.

*   *   *

I deliberately put only one image into *Orphée*. After the performance it is quoted back at me.

To miss any one line in *Orphée* except that image, is to lose a bolt from the machine; it will no longer work.

After the school of botching comes the school of stage-realism. Now there is no question of living on the stage; it is a question of making the stage live.

This truth of the theatre is the poetry of the theatre, truer than the true.

Just as the speed of *Orphée* is too broken up for a spectator reared on plays that have been refurbished like old scenery, so to a mind accustomed to plays built like a real house, the house of *Orphée* looks like a mad-house.

*　　　　　*　　　　　*

"Why are your name and address in the mouth of Orphée's bust?"

It is the portrait of the donor at the bottom of the canvas, the name of the person who has been run over being questioned at the chemist's shop.

*　　　　　*　　　　　*

One can find evidence of the singular perspective of the theatre even in the so-called 'realist' theatre. Lucien Guitry told me that in one of his plays, dining at the Ritz with another character, he had the dinner sent in from Larue's. Despite all his efforts the scene sending in the dinner along with the maître d'hôtel. He replaced this maître d'hôtel by an actor and at once obtained the right perspective.

Choreographers, then, arrange your dance to some famous piece of music (CARMEN, TRISTAN AND ISOLDE, anything) and take it away afterwards.

Ask the painter to be a stage-director.

The bath of the Graces in "Mercure"[1] is a stage-setting. Build on pantomime, the tableau vivant, the silent gesture. Stop being frivolous and conjugating the arts.

*   *   *

We are in a period of such individualism that one no longer speaks of disciples; one speaks of thieves.

*   *   *

The only outcome of an increasingly pronounced individualism is solitude. Now it is no longer artists from the other bank of the river who detest each other, but artists from the same bank, men who share the same solitude, the same cell, who exploit the same square foot of excavation. It is that which makes our worst enemy the only one who will be capable of understanding us completely, and vice versa.

*   *   *

CHOOSING ONE'S SNARES

The rhythm of our life goes in phases, which are all alike, except that they occur in a way which renders them unrecognisable. The event which constitutes a snare, or the person, are all the more dangerous because, for their own part, they follow

[1] This ballet was first produced for Comte Etienne de Beaumont's *Soirées de Paris* in 1924. The music was by Erik Satie, the décor by Picasso and the choreography by Massine. (Tr.)

the same law and wear their mask with all sincerity.

Ultimately, suffering gives us a warning and indicates many snares. But, unless one refuses to live insipidly, one must accept certain snares, despite the certain knowledge that they bring fatal consequences. It is wise to be foolish, when circumstances make the effort worthwhile. Goethe was one of the first to speak of an artistic truth being obtained by the reverse of reality (*à propos* an engraving by Rembrandt). To-day, all research is admitted in so far as it is research. It is difficult to imagine the solitude of Uccello. "This poor Paolo," said Vasari, "little versed in the science of horsemanship, would have produced a master-piece, if he had not represented his horse lifting two legs on the same side, which is impossible." Yet all the nobility of the work of which Vasari speaks arises from this 'counter-pace,' from this total entry on the part of the artist, which is a self-affirmation and a cry across the centuries: *This horse is a pretext. It prevents me from dying. I am here!*

*　　　　*　　　　*

THE INTENSITY OF AN ATMOSPHERE

Typical theatre atmosphere—the courtyard of an inn; chorus of scullions; the coach arrives. Some of the leading members of the cast alight. One guesses that the actors and actresses are speaking amongst themselves about something other than the play. Evening falls. The orchestra takes up again, in muted tones, the scullions' chorus.

I want to recapture that atmosphere. If I do, there will be no courtyard, no coach, no evening falling, no scullions' chorus.

For example, it is the fact that the actors in the Châtelet Theatre have to speak loudly, which made me discover the loudspeaker style of *Les Mariés de la Tour Eiffel*.[1]

The text of *Les Mariés*. I wanted the heavy phrases in the text to sound as if one were seeing postcards of the Venus de Milo, Millet's *Angélus* and the *Gioconda* side by side

*　　　*　　　*

Apart from my intimate memories of the theatre, three outstanding stage-sets remain in my mind. The wreck and the hold-up of the train in *Le Tour du Monde en 80 Jours, Le Dit des Jeux du Monde*, designed by Fauconnet at the Vieux-Colombier and *Couleur du Temps* designed by Vlaminck at the Renée Maubel Theatre.

*　　　*　　　*

There are too many improvements, too much comfort in life. How sad it will be when the enormous, warm, rich whisper is suppressed, when the places where the talking film no longer talks are gone and the contrast between the visual platitude and the auditory perspective disappears.

[1] Cocteau's play, with music by *Les Six*, was first performed in 1921 (Tr.)

When everything has been brought into focus—perspective, colour and sound, the young will ransack this sham theatre and will wisely make use of the delightful old mistakes, which have been overcome by luxury, business, and the inevitable "comfort" of science. (Those little hotels which are ruined as soon as the proprietor earns enough to make them look like his dreams, although they deserve to be successful, which amazes him, for he cannot see why).

*　　　　*　　　　*

I have read the Victor Hugo file in the Comédie-Française. On a little piece of paper he decides where his young friends will sit, notes the lines which must be applauded, arranges his *claque* and *counter-claque*.

And we are always accused of being organisers! We have only counted on the unknown friends with whom we are so often reproached, who surprise us with their support. These young friends of Hugo must have been the fine flower of the avant-garde. Except for Pétrus Borel I do not know a single name.

pany with his idol. He was on duty at his post, with his grotesque beard, nostrils and waistcoat.

*　　　　*　　　　*

One would rather like to make Hugo smoke. Victor Hugo lacked nothing, except illness. I am wrong.

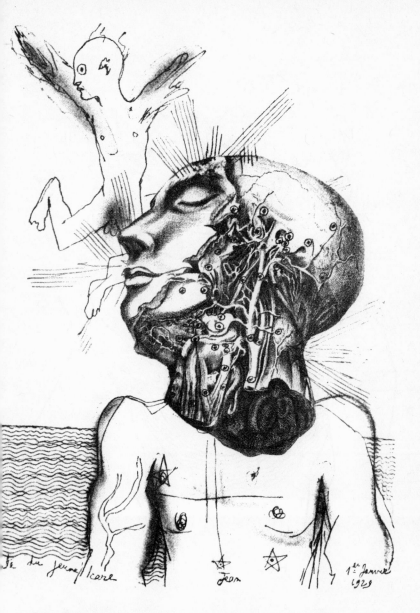

14   *The fall of young Icarus 1st January, 1929*

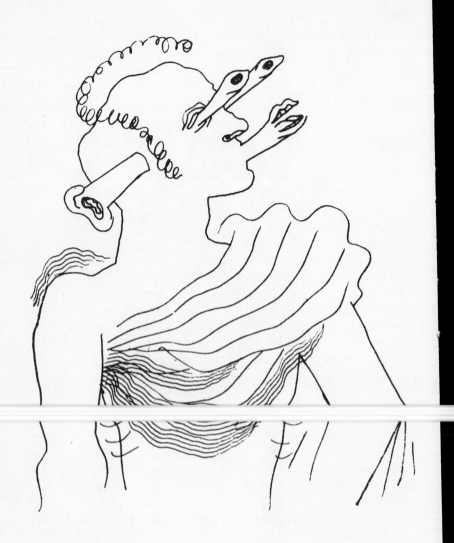

15   *Drawing*

His illness made his reputation. He was mad. At first megalomaniac, then mad. (His drawings, furniture, love affairs and methods of work bear this out).

*   *   *

The element of novelty in a work is always ill-fated. One only sees the work when the novelty becomes banal and disappears. Victor Hugo's period, which was very vulgar, forced him to break superficially with the accepted forms. The element of novelty remains in the foreground. This highlighting has become a platitude: his theatre survives because we have a strong stomach.

Imagine a man, seated at his table, writing *Cromwell* as a side-line to his work. Péguy, who was an admirer of Hugo, enumerated his works to me.

"There must be more," he repeated. "Let's see, let's see!" he recapitulated and he searched. He had forgotten *Les Misérables*.

*   *   *

Nothing more abnormal than a poet who approximates to the normal man: Hugo or Goethe . . . This is the madman at large. The madman who does not appear mad. The madman who is never suspect. When I wrote that Victor Hugo was a madman who believed himself to be Victor Hugo, I was not joking. Is not the arch-sin against wit to be witty? This was no sally, this was a synthesis; the outline of a study which I refuse to write and which others will write one day. The role of the poet is not to prove but to affirm without producing any of the encumbering evidence which he possesses; this is the basis of his affirmation. In the course of time, the slow discovery of this evidence gives the poet his place as a seer. In Guernsey Hugo's madness was directed towards furniture and photography. He was photographed twenty or thirty times a day. Hugo without a beard! What an admission! There is always a period when a man with a beard shaves it off. This period does not last. He returns headlong to his beard.

*   *   *

Hugo (during the case of *Le Roi S'Amuse*): *today censorship, tomorrow exile!* This exclamation makes one think. This exile must have been prepared a long time ahead.

*   *   *

Sacred monsters like Goethe and Victor Hugo are

Oscar Wilde any more: he would pall.

*   *   *

Speed prevents one from remaining stationary round a face. Although Barrès was hypnotised by this race of men, he still obtained something of this kind. He is without doubt the last example of a vanished type. Chesterton describes this phenomenon very well à propos Dickens.

*　　　　*　　　　*

The notorious distortions due to opium. Slowness, laziness, inactive dreams. *Opéra*[1] is the work of an opium addict. "You said it," reply the imbeciles. Now I have never reached such speeds. Speeds which attain immobility. My electric fan makes no draught and does not disturb the picture placed behind it, but I do not advise anyone to put their finger in it.

*　　　　*　　　　*

To reproach me with the puns in *Opéra* is to confuse puns with coincidences. *Opéra* is a slot-machine for distributing oracles, a talking bust, an oracular book. I dig. My spade encounters some hard object. I uncover and clean it. *L'Ami Zamore de Madame du Barry* was inevitable and that is no play on words.

*　　　　*　　　　*

One always speaks of the slavery of opium. The regularity it imposes on the passing hours is not only a discipline, it is also a liberation. Liberation from visits and from people sitting round in circles.

[1] Cocteau published this book of poems in 1927 (Tr.)

I would add that opium is the opposite of the Pravaz syringe. It reassures. It reassures by reason of its luxury, its rites, the anti-medical elegance of its lamps, furnaces, pipes and the age-old perfection of this exquisite poisoning.

*   *   *

Even without any spirit of proselytising, it is impossible for a person who does not smoke to live with a person who does. Each would inhabit a different world. One of the few protections against a relapse will then be a sense of responsibility.

*   *   *

For two months I have been discharging bile. The yellow race: bile implanted in the blood.

Opium is a decision to be taken. Our only error is wanting to smoke and to share the privileges of those who do not smoke. It is rare for an addict to forsake opium. Opium forsakes him, ruining everything. It is a substance which escapes analysis—

against the smoker. It is the barometer of a diseased sensibility. At times when the weather is humid, the pipe drips. If an addict goes to the sea-side, the drug swells and refuses to burn. The approach of snow, a storm or the mistral, destroys its efficacy. Some noisy surroundings can take away all its virtues.

54

In short, there is no mistress more exacting than this drug which takes jealousy to the point of emasculating the addict.

*　　　　*　　　　*

In preparing raw opium the alkaloids are combined quite haphazardly. It is impossible to foresee the consequences. By adding the dross one increases the chances of success, but risks destroying a masterpiece. It is the beat of a gong which breaks the melody. I do not recommend a drop of port or *fine champagne*. I recommend a litre of old red wine in the water in which the raw pill is soaking, afterwards avoid bringing it to the boil, strain seven times and keep at it for eight days.

*　　　　*　　　　*

If he takes care of himself, an addict who inhales twelve pipes a day all his life will not only be fortified against influenza, colds and sore throats, but will also be far less in danger than a man who drinks a glass of brandy or who smokes four cigars. I know people who have smoked one, three, seven, up to twelve pipes a day for forty years.

*　　　　*　　　　*

Some people will say to you: "The discriminating

throw away the dross." Others: "The discriminating make their boys smoke while they smoke only the dross." If one questions a boy about the drug's dangers, "Good drug make fat," he replies. "Dross make sick."

The vice of opium-smoking is to smoke the dross.

*　　　*　　　*

Just as one must not confuse a cure and its typhoid-like convalescence with a suppression by means of various substitutes (physical exercise, walking, winter-sports, cocaine or alcohol), so one must not confuse addiction with habit. Some people only smoke on Sundays. On Sundays they cannot do without the drug; that is habit. Addiction ruins the liver, affects the nervous cells, causes constipation, makes the temples like parchment and contracts the iris of the eye. Habit is a rhythm, a singular hunger which can upset the addict, but causes him no harm.

The symptoms of the craving are of so strange a kind that they cannot be described. Only the nurses in clinics succeed in forming some impression. (The

that the earth is turning a little less fast, that the moon is coming a little closer.

*　　　*　　　*

A wheel is a wheel. Opium is opium. Every other luxury is mere ingenuity; as if man, not knowing the wheel, had made the first carriage, after the style of a horse, with mechanical legs.

*   *   *

Let us profit from insomnia to attempt the impossible: to describe the craving.

Byron said: "Love cannot withstand seasickness." Like love, like seasickness, the craving penetrates everywhere. Resistance is useless. At first a malaise, then things become worse. Imagine a silence equivalent to the crying of thousands of children whose mothers do not return to give them the breast. The lover's anxiety transposed into nervous awareness. An absence which dominates, a negative despotism.

The phenomena become clearer. Flashes like moiré before the eyes, champagne in the veins, frozen siphons, cramps, sweating at the root of the hair, dryness in the mouth, sniffling, tears. Do not persist. Your courage is to no purpose. If you delay too long, you will no longer be able to take your equipment and roll your pipe. Smoke. Your body was waiting only for a sign. One pipe is enough.

*   *   *

It is easy to say: "Opium arrests life, anaesthetises. Well-being comes from a kind of death."

Without opium I am cold, I catch cold, I do not feel hungry. I am impatient to impose what I invent. When I smoke, I am warm, I do not know what colds

are, I am hungry, my impatience disappears. Doctors,
reflect on this riddle!

*   *   *

Scholars are not curious, said France. He is right.

*   *   *

Opium is the 'femme fatale,' the pagodas, the
lanterns! I do not have the strength to undeceive
you. Since science does not know how to distinguish
between the curative and the destructive properties
of opium, I must yield to it. Never have I regretted
more profoundly not having been a poet and a
doctor, like Apollo.

*   *   *

We all carry within us something folded up like
those Japanese flowers made of wood which unfold
in water.
Opium plays the same role as the water. None of

a person who does not smoke may never know the
kind of flower that opium might have unfolded
within him. One must not take opium too seriously.
About 1909 there were artists who smoked without
talking about it and who no longer smoke. Many
young couples smoke without anyone suspecting it;
colonials smoke to combat fever and stop smoking

Per la
boca de.
su
herida

16 *Through the mouth of his wound*

17 Drawing

18 Drawing

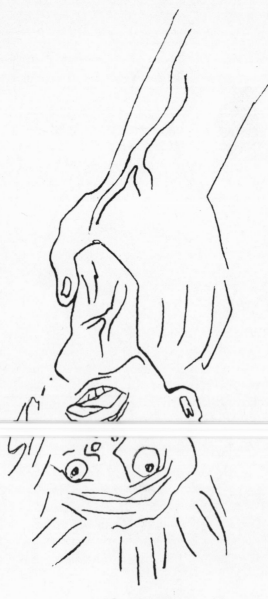

19 Drawing

when circumstances force them to stop. They then experience the discomforts of a heavy dose of influenza. Opium spares all these addicts because they did not and do not take it seriously.

Opium becomes serious to the extent to which it affects the nerve centres which control the soul. Otherwise, it is an antidote, a pleasure, an ultimate siesta.

The danger is smoking as a defence against some moral disequilibrium. Then it is difficult to approach the drug in the way it must be approached, as wild beasts should be approached—without fear.

*   *   *

One day, when I was in fact cured, and was attempting to unravel a little the vexed problem of opium with Dr. Z. (more fitted by his youth to overcome established practices), Dr. X. (of the generation of the great unbelievers) asked my nurse if he could come to see me. "He's with Dr. Z . . ," she replied. "Oh, then, since they're talking about literature, I shan't go up. I'm not equal to it."

*   *   *

My nurse (a Breton woman) said: "One cannot hold it against the Blessed Virgin for having deceived the good Lord, because he had gone off to make war on the Jews and left her all the time all alone."

There is one kind nurse, a war widow from the

North. At table her colleagues question her about the German occupation during the war. They sip their coffee and wait for the horrors.

"They were very kind," she replies, "they used to share their crusts of bread with my little boy and even if one of them did behave incorrectly, one did not dare to complain to the Kommandatura, because they were punished too severely. If they pestered a woman they were tied to a tree for two days."

This reply dismays the table. The widow is suspect. She is called the Boche. She cries and little by little she changes her memories, she slips in a little horror. She wants to live.

*　　　　*　　　　*

The Comtesse de H . . . , a German of Swedish origin, occupies the corner room. I can see her windows. The nurses have asked the matron to transfer the widow from the North away from the Comtesse's room. "She is in with the Germans. They could easily be plotting together!"

*　　　　*　　　　*

This morning, the day of Foch's funeral, the Comtesse opens her window as usual. "She is defying us," say the staff.

*　　　　*　　　　*

The south wing of the former Hôtel Pozzo di Borgo was built in 1914 by a German medical firm. Alas! the walls are papier mâché. If one drives in a nail, the room falls to pieces. My nurse shows me three sunbathing balconies: "Look, the devils," she says, "they made platforms for shelling Paris."

*　　　　*　　　　*

While I am drawing, E . . , who is a replacement, is writing to her brother: "I'm taking advantage of the fact that my patient has found a pastime for the moment in writing to you." She pronounces the word *Quiès* (ear-plugs called Quiès) *Cuisses* (thighs). Mlle d'A . . . would never have been able to go to sleep without putting her Cuisses in her ears.

Do not forget that no visitors are allowed, that a nervous case, a semi-lunatic who ought to be entertained, is shut up alone with his nurse for months on end. The chief medical officer comes in for a minute. If the patient is all right, he stays longer. If the patient is not well, he beats a retreat. The psychiatrist attached to the establishment is young, agreeable and lively. He cannot help but be liked. If he is liked, a long visit vexes the chief medical officer, who is disliked. He stays ten minutes.

Any nurse is allotted to any patient. Yet the choice of a nurse is of paramount importance for nervous cases. Smiles: "Ah! If we also had to worry about details like that . . ." And the nervous patient is treated like an old dodderer. The composition of the medicines is kept hidden from him. Human contacts are avoided. The doctor must be inhuman. The doctor who talks and makes contact with the patient is never taken seriously. "Yes, he's a good talker, but if I were very ill I should send for someone else." Psychology is the enemy of medicine. Rather than tackle the question of opium with the patient who is obsessed by it, they avoid it. A real doctor does not stay long in the room, he conceals his tricks for lack of tricks. This method has corrupted the patients. They suspect the doctor who listens to them, the human doctor. Dr. M. has killed all my family and treated my brother's broken nose for erysipelas. His frock coat and bald pate were re-assuring.

*   *   *

Opium perpetuates itself across the centuries like the royal cubit. Helen of Troy knew recipes as long-lost as the mysteries of the Great Pyramid. Gradually, they are all brought together again: Ronsard tries

alarming poem. He knew a Helen: he no longer knew how to prepare the poppy.

*   *   *

I am not one of the cured who is proud of his effort. I am ashamed to have been expelled from that world, compared with which the world of health resembles those revolting films in which ministers unveil statues.

*   *   *

It is hard to feel oneself dismissed by opium after several failures: it is hard to know that this magic carpet exists and that one will no longer fly on it; it was pleasant to buy it, as in the Baghdad of the Caliphs, from the Chinese in a sordid street hung with washing; pleasant to return home quickly to try it out in one's hotel, in the room between the columns where George Sand and Chopin lived, to unroll it, stretch out on it, open the window on to the port, and take off. Undoubtedly too pleasant.

*   *   *

The addict becomes as one with the objects which surround him. His cigarette, a finger, falls from his hand.

*   *   *

The addict is surrounded with slopes. Impossible to keep the spirit on the heights. It is 11 o'clock in the evening. One smokes for five minutes; one looks at one's watch: it is five o'clock in the morning.

*   *   *

Countless times the addict must return to his

point of departure as the ball in the rifle range returns to the trough. The slightest untimely noise blows the egg off the fountain.

*   *   *

Grey matter and brown matter make the best harmony.

The addict's optimism is not a drunkard's optimism. It emulates the optimism of health.

*   *   *

Picasso used to say to me: *The smell of opium is the least stupid smell in the world.* The only smell one can compare with it is that of a circus or a sea port.

Raw opium. If you do not shut it up in a metal chest but content yourself with a box, the black serpent will soon have crept out. Be warned! It hugs the walls, goes down the stairs and the floors, turns, crosses the hall, go down the arcnway and will soon coil itself round the policeman's neck.

*   *   *

To speak of "drugs" when talking of opium amounts to confusing Pommard with Pernod.

My room was previously occupied by a naval

officer who looked after three bodies and changed legs at top speed.

When I draw, the nurse says to me: "You frighten me, you have a murderer's face!"

I would not like to be taken by surprise when I am writing. I have always drawn. Writing for me is drawing, tying the lines together in such a way that they make writing, or undoing them in such a way that the writing becomes drawing. I do not go beyond that. I write, I try to outline exactly the profile of an idea, of an action. In short, I encircle phantoms, I find the contours of emptiness, I draw.

*　　　*　　　*

To make mystery luminous (mysterious, obscure mystery—a pleonasm) and so to restore to it the purity of mystery. *Meine Nacht ist Licht* . . .

To create: to destroy everything around one which prevents one from projecting oneself in time through the agency of some appearance, the purpose of this appearance being no more than a subterfuge for making oneself visible after death.

*　　　*　　　*

SURPRISES AT THE COURT OF GOD

A little girl steals cherries. The whole of her long life is spent in atoning for this lapse, by prayer. The good woman dies. GOD: *You have been chosen because you stole cherries.*

The story of the fig-tree from which Jesus, being hungry, demands figs when they are not in season and on which he takes revenge. Jesus is about to die. Only a few days remain to him. He no longer speaks; he counts his gestures. His gesture, in blasting the innocent tree of which he asks the impossible demands to be understood in the same way as those works which appear obscure because they are concise. It has nothing to do with the absurd discretion of kings.

One must make an end to the myth of opium—visions. Opium nourishes a state of half-dream. It puts the emotions to sleep, exalts the heart and lightens the spirit.

Unless one gets drunk on it as on anything else, I do not find that it has any sacrilegious virtue. Its only fault is ultimately to make one ill. But it happens that one catches one's death in church.

If the road is straight from the church to God, I recommend the Chablis road, which is always empty, on a Christmas night.

*　　　*　　　*

THE DESIGNS OF MY PEN
THE OBSCURE DESIGNS OF PROVIDENCE

A pure spirit has neither a beginning nor an end and it never changes. The fall of the angels is there-

66

20   Night of December 30th, 1928

21   *Night of December 31st, 1928*

fore senseless. I mean that it is lacking in sense to the extent that it recalls films being run backwards. The devil represents in some way the shortcomings of God. Without the devil God would be inhuman.

There are devils in Saint-Sulpice.

De Quincey astonishes me when he speaks of his walks and his visits to the Opera. For it needs only a change of position, or a change of light, to destroy the whole edifice of calm.

Smoking *à deux* is already crowded. Smoking *à trois* is difficult. Smoking *à quatre* is impossible.

Disgusted by literature, I wanted to go beyond it and live my work. The result is that my work is consuming me, that it is beginning to live, and I to die. Moreover, works divide themselves into two: those which bring to life; those which kill.

One day, one of our writers whom I used to reproach with writing best-sellers and with never expressing himself, led me in front of a mirror.

"I want to be strong," he said. "Look at yourself. I want to eat. I want to travel. I want to live. I do not want to become a fountain-pen."

A thinking reed! A suffering reed! A bleeding reed! That's it! In short I have reached this sinister conclusion: the penalty for not wanting to become a man of letters is to become a fountain-pen.

*   *   *

Nervous people (normal) fade out in the evening. Nervous people (opium-addicts) light up in the evening. Here I find any book good, provided the attendants supply me. I read *Le Fils de d'Artagnan* by Paul Féval *fils*. Suddenly, Athos and the son of d'Artagnan meet face to face. I cry. I feel no shame about these tears. Then I come across this phrase. "The blood-stained face was covered over with a mask of black velvet etc . . .'

What? Does the Baron de Souvré, after his struggles and soakings, still wear his mask? Naturally, Souvré wears a mask of black velvet. That is his character. That is the secret of Fantomas' greatness. Writers of epics are no more concerned about wigs and wrong dates than Homer with geography and metamorphoses.

One must be cured not of opium but of intelligence. Since 1924 I have only kept the works I wrote as a prisoner.

*   *   *

Books must have fire and shadow. The shadows change their position. At sixteen one devours *Dorian Gray*. Afterwards, the book becomes ridiculous. I happened to pick it up again and find in it some very beautiful shadows (the episode of Sybil Vane's brother) and to see how unjust one is. In certain books the shadows do not move; they dance on the same spot. *Moll Flanders, Manon, Pan, La Chartreuse, Splendeurs et Misères, Genji.*

All the official critics said that *Thomas l'Impos-*

teur[1] described an unreal war and that one could easily see that I had never been involved. In fact, there is no single landscape, no single scene in this book, which I have not inhabited or lived. The sub-title: *histoire*, had two meanings.

They take that snow placed between the earth and Thomas' feet, that dream-like gait, for a triviality in bad taste. An insult to the 'tommy.'

I left the war when I realised, one night at Nieuport, that I was enjoying myself. That disgusted me. I had forgotten hatred, justice and the other humbug. I had let myself be carried away by friendship, danger and surprises, I was living in the clouds. Hardly had I made this discovery when I prepared to leave, taking advantage of being ill. This I concealed, like children playing.

We poets have a mania for truth, we attempt to report in detail what strikes us. 'That's enough of the "you" style,' is the praise which our accuracy always earns. One can imagine the credit earned by the honesty of our reports about what we alone see, by the admiring incredulity aroused by our accuracy about everyday sights that everyone can see.

The poet never asks for admiration; he wants to be believed.

*   *   *

Everything that is not believed remains background.

[1] Cocteau's novel recently translated into English, titled *The Impostor*. (published by Peter Owen)

*   *   *

Beauty moves quickly, slowly. It baffles by this blending of irreconcilables. Perspective gives to this inhuman mixture a false air of humanity, an air of the possible, the noble. Thanks to this compromise, the public believes it can hear and see the classics.

*   *   *

The slow speed of opium. Under the influence of opium one becomes the meeting place for the phenomena which art sends to us from outside.

The addict can become a masterpiece. A masterpiece which is above discussion. A perfect masterpiece, because it is fugitive, without form and without judges.

*   *   *

However great the individualism, the solitary, reserved, luxurious, monstrous side of the masterpiece, it is no less social, no less capable of affecting ....., ...g and ....g a crowd of people spiritually and materially.

Now the need for self-expression, for contact with the outside world, disappears with the hedonist.

He does not seek to create masterpieces, he seeks to become one himself, the most unknown, the most egotistical.

To say of an addict who is in a continual state of

70

euphoria that he is degrading himself is like saying of marble that it is spoilt by Michelangelo, of canvas that it is stained by Raphael, of paper that it is soiled by Shakespeare, of silence that it is broken by Bach.

Nothing less impure than this masterpiece, an opium-addict. Nothing more natural than society demanding a share, condemning him like an invisible beauty without the shadow of prostitution.

* * *

The painter who likes to paint trees, becoming a tree. Children carry within them a natural drug. The death of Thomas the Impostor is a case of the child playing at horses turning into a horse.

All children possess the magic power of being able to change themselves into what they wish. Poets, in whom childhood is prolonged, suffer a great deal when they lose this power. This is undoubtedly one of the reasons which drives the poet to use opium.

* * *

A memory strikes me. When, after the trial of Satie (he had been sending insulting post-cards), I abandoned myself to 'threats of violence against a lawyer in the exercise of his functions,' I did not realise for one second the consequences of my act. It was an act of passion. The present absorbs us completely. Our psyche contracts until it becomes a dot. No more past, no more future.

The past and the future torment me and the acts of passion are rare. Now opium stirs up the past and the future, making them a present whole. It is the negative of passion.

Alcohol provokes fits of madness.

Opium provokes fits of wisdom.

*   *   *

DOGS. Satie wanted to make a theatre for dogs. The curtain rises. The set consists of a bone.

*   *   *

In England they have just made a film for dogs. The hundred and fifty dogs who were invited hurled themselves at the screen and tore it to pieces. (N. Y. Times).

*   *   *

When I was staying at no. 45, rue La Bruyère with

for tidiness, I went out for a walk (I was then fourteen) with a fox-terrier of a year and a half old, which was just tolerated. At the bottom of the white steps in the hall my terrier arched his back and relieved himself. I rushed forward, ready to strike him. Agony dilated the poor beast's eyes; he ate his droppings and sat up begging.

*   *   *

At the clinic, at five o'clock, the old bull-dog who is dying is given a fatal injection of morphine. One hour later he is playing in the garden, jumping and rolling about. The following day, at five, he scratched at the doctor's door and asked for his injection.

*   *   *

Madame de C's dog, at Grasse, in love with the bitch belonging to Marie C . : , who lives some miles away. He watches out for a tram and jumps on the platform. The same performance coming back.

*   *   *

On the boulevards Madame A. D . . . had been sold a tiny dog. She came home and put the dog down while she went for some water. She came back and found the dog perched on a picture frame. It was a rat in dog's skin. Out of anger he had succeeded in gnawing away his false paws.

*   *   *

The Duc de L . . . paid the castle caretakers to look after his old poodle. One day he arrived unexpectedly. A yellow dog ran towards him dragging a white poodle's skin behind him. For three years the caretakers had disguised their own dog in the skin of the dead one.

If an addict who has been completely cured starts smoking again he no longer experiences the discomforts of his first addiction. There exists, therefore, outside alkaloids and habit, a sense for opium, an intangible habit which lives on, despite the recasting of the organism. This sense must not be taken for the regret felt by an opium-addict who has become normal again, although this regret does constitute part of the appeal. The dead drug leaves a ghost behind. At certain hours it haunts the house.

*   *   *

An addict who has been cured keeps defences against the poison within himself. If he becomes addicted again his defences come into action and force him to take stronger doses than those of his first addiction.

*   *   *

trom changes in the weather. He never catches cold. He suffers only from the changes in drugs, doses and hours, in everything in fact which influences the barometer of opium.

Opium has its colds, shivers and fevers which do not coincide with cold and heat.

*   *   *

Doctors would have us believe that opium dulls us and takes away our sense of values. But if opium takes away the old scale of values from under our feet, it sets up another for us, superior and more delicate.

*   *   *

(1930). One cannot say that opium, by removing all sexual obsessions, weakens the smoker, because not only does it not cause impotence, but what is more it replaces those somewhat base obsessions by others which are somewhat lofty, very strange and unknown to a sexually normal organism.

For instance a type of mind will be sensed, sought out, and linked across the centuries and the arts, against all appearances, and will haunt the untended sexuality across the most dissimilar sexes and social backgrounds (Dargelos, Agathe, the stars and the boxers in Paul's bedroom).

*   *   *

All animals are charmed by opium. Addicts in the colonies know the danger of this bait for wild beasts and reptiles.

Flies gather round the tray and dream, the lizards with their little mittens swoon on the ceiling above the lamp and wait for the night, mice come close and nibble the dross. I do not speak of the dogs and monkeys who become addicted like their masters.

At Marseilles, among the Annamites, where one smokes with implements calculated to confuse the police (a gas-pipe, a sample bottle of benedictine with a hole in it, and a hat-pin), the cockroaches and the spiders form a circle in ecstasy.

*   *   *

A POOR TYPE. THIS UNINTERESTING CREATURE. Labels which would be attached by the newspapers and the police to all those whom we love and admire. Leonardo da Vinci, for example.

In addition there are certain superior cliché remarks made by the people who know. *But the young Annamites do not smoke. In Indo-China the people don't smoke any longer. It's only in books that they smoke aboard ship.*

When I hear one of these phrases I close my eyes, I see again the boys' berths on board the X., one of the largest steamers on the Marseilles-Saïgon line. The X was waiting to get under way. The purser, one of my opium-smoking frie̶n̶d̶s̶ ̶h̶a̶d̶ ̶o̶f̶f̶e̶r̶e̶d̶ ̶h̶i̶s̶
̶e̶s̶c̶a̶p̶a̶d̶e̶ ̶t̶o̶ ̶m̶e̶. At eleven o'clock at night we crossed the deserted docks and climbed up the ladder on to the deck. We had to follow our guide at full speed and avoid the watch. We climbed over cables, worked round columns and Greek temples, crossed public squares, labyrinths of machines, shadow and moon-light, we mixed up the companion ways and the corridors so much and so well that our poor guide

began to lose his head, until. softly, that powerful strange smell put us on the right path.

Imagine enormous berths, four or five dormitories, where sixty 'boys' lay smoking on two tiers of planks. In each dormitory a long table filled up the empty space. Standing on these tables, and cut in two by a flat, unmoving cloud half-way up the room, the late-comers were undressing, tying up the cords where they liked to hang up their washing, and gently rubbing their shoulders.

The scene was lit by the dim lights of the lamps, and on top of them burnt the spluttering drug. The bodies were wedged against each other and without causing the slightest surprise, or the slightest ungraciousness, we took our places where there was really no place left, with our legs doubled up and our heads resting on stools. The noise we made did not even disturb one of the boys who was sleeping with his head against mine. A nightmare convulsed him; he had sunk to the bottom of the sleep that stifled him, entering into him through his mouth, his large nostrils and the ears which stuck out from his head. His swollen face was closed like an angry fist, he sweated, turned over and tore at his silken rags. He looked as though a stroke of the lancet would deliver him and bring forth the nightmare. His grimaces formed an extraordinary contrast with the calm of the others, a vegetable calm, a calm which reminded me of something familiar. What was it? On those planks lay the twisted bodies in which the skeletons, visible through the pale skin, were no more than the delicate armatures of a dream . . . In fact, it was the olive trees of Provence which those young sleepers evoked in me, the twisted olive trees on the flat red earth, their silver clouds hanging in the air.

In that place I could almost believe that it was all this profound lightness that alone kept this most monumental ship floating on the water.

*   *   *

I wanted to take notes during my stay in the clinic and above all to contradict myself in order to follow the stages of the treatment. It was a question of talking about opium without embarrassment, without literature and without any medical knowledge.[1]

The specialists seem to be unaware of the world which separates the opium addict from the other victims of poisons, 'the drug,' and drugs.

I am not trying to defend the drug; I am trying to see clearly in the dark, to make blunders and to come face to face with the problems which are always approached from the side.

shake off the yoke, to revolt against the ridiculous prejudices and follow new developments.

A strange thing. Our physical safety accepts doctors who correspond to the artists whom our moral safety rejects. Imagine being cared for by someone like Ziem, Henner or Jean Aicard.

[1] Consult *Le Livre de la Feuemée* by Louis Laloy, the only good modern work on opium.

Will the young doctors discover either an active type of cure (the present method remains passive), or a regime which would enable us to withstand the blessings of the poppy?

The medical faculty detests intuition or risks; it wants practitioners, forgetting that they only arise thanks to discoveries which in the first place come up against scepticism, one of the worst forms of comfort.

There will be objections—art and science follow different paths. This is not true.

*　　　　*　　　　*

A normal man, from the sexual point of view, should be capable of making love with anyone and even with anything, because the instinct of the species is blind; it works in the mass. This explains the casual behaviour of the people and above all of sailors, which is usually attributed to vice. Only the sexual act counts. A brute is little concerned with the circumstances which provoke it. I do not speak of love.

Vice begins with choice. According to the heredity, intelligence and nervous fatigue of the subject concerned, this choice becomes more and more selective to the point of becoming inexplicable, comic or criminal.

*　　　　*　　　　*

A mother who says 'My son will only marry a

blonde,' does not suspect that her remark corresponds to the worst sexual imbroglios. Travesties, mingling of the sexes, torturing of animals, chains and insults.

*   *   *

STRANGE LACK OF INTEREST IN SEX THROUGH THE EXISTENCE OF A SPIRITUAL PROGENY

Art is born of coitus between the male and female elements of which we are all composed, and they are more balanced in the case of artists than of other men. It results from a kind of incest, of love of self for self, of parthenogenesis. It is this that makes marriage so dangerous among artists, for whom it represents a pleonasm, a monstrous effort towards the norm. The 'poor specimen' look which is the mark of so many men of genius arises from the fact that the creative instinct is satisfied elsewhere and leaves sexual pleasure free to exert itself in the pure domain of aesthetics, inclining it also towards unfruitful forms of expression.

*   *

One cannot translate a real poet; not because his style is musical, but because his thought has a plastic quality, and, if this changes, the thought changes.

A Russian said to me: 'The style of *Orphée* is musical in the opposite way to what the public calls musical. In spite of its lack of music, it is musical because it leaves the spirit free to profit from it as it wishes.'

*　　　*　　　*

A poet, unless he is a politician (such as Hugo, Shelley or Byron), must only count on readers who know his language, the spirit of his language and the soul of his language.

*　　　*　　　*

The crowd likes works which impose their melody, which hypnotise, which hypertrophy its sensibility to the point of putting the critical sense to sleep. The crowd is feminine; it likes to obey or bite.

*　　　*　　　*

Radiguet said *'The public asks us if the author is serious. I ask the public if they are serious.'* Alas! works of genius demand a public of genius. One can achieve a substitute for this receptive state of genius through the electricity emanating from an agglomeration of mediocre persons. This substitute allows one to have illusions about the fate of a play in the theatre.

*　　　*　　　*

Ever since 1870 artists have been getting used to

despising the public. The stupidity of the public is admitted. This prejudice risks falling into the same category as the public's prejudices. Like the absurd prejudice against the Comédie Française, the Opéra, the Opéra Comique, the theatres of all the famous scandals.

For those who seek problems to solve, is there not one here? Formerly genius reached the public with slowness, concessions, even intermediaries. One should study the public and discover the card trick which would deceive it over fast-moving works.

The cinema has thawed out people's brains. At Dullin's we moved an audience of ordinary people two hundred times by means of *Antigone*[1] (the play lasts forty minutes) played at full speed and with no other theme except the love between brother and sister. This audience did not know Sophocles.

*   *   *

What of a poet or a dramatist endowed with the Indian fakir's power of mass-hypnosis? Why do you ... the realm of illusion and of seeing the trick behind the curtain? It is a case of people making fun of genius because they cannot be touched by it. That is the whole difference between us and the camera with its cow-eye. Many minds are confused between being touched and being victimised, admiring and being the dupe. They

[1] Cocteau's free adaption of Sophocles' play was first produced in 1922 with music by Honegger. (Tr.)

22 Drawing

23 **Through the mouth of his wound**

brace themselves against hypnosis. It is easy, alas! because the poet uses his fluid indirectly and possesses only the feeblest means of persuasion.

A museum is only justified to the extent that it bears witness to ancient activities, and keeps what remains of the phosphorescence around works, the fluid that emanates from them, and thanks to which they succeed in overcoming death.

*   *   *

Stendhal was perfectly right when he said that a woman entered a carriage with genius. The use of the word "genius" offends our reluctance to give praise.

For a creative artist—a painter for example—is most lavish with his genius in certain farces, charades, and improvised disguises which make him suspect to duller wits; he expresses himself through them without resorting to any of the calculations or dead matter indispensable to the survival of a work of art.

It is the burning moment of lyricism, this conflagration (free of all the boredom which fascinates the solemn imbecile) that Picasso succeeds in capturing in certain of his works.

*   *   *

One never comes to the end. If Picasso, in one of his anti-painting moods, were to jump out of the window, Mr. X . . , the brilliant collector, would say: *"That makes a lovely mark,"* he would buy the pavement and have it framed *in a false window,* by Z . . , the brilliant frame-maker. Picasso, the painter of crucifixions. The canvases which result from his fits of rage against painting (torn linen, nails, rope, gall) in which the painter crucifies himself, crucifies painting, spits on it, spears it, finds himself check-mated, and fatally forced to accept the fact that the whole massacre must end in a guitar.

My dream, in music, would be to hear *the music of Picasso's guitars.*

*   *   *

(April 1930). In the midst of the blue sky, erect on a globe like the Hindu world resting on the elephant and the tortoises, worlds which are people of flesh and bone, pink carcases, monsters of solitude and love.

*   *   *

..... an audience scandal. It arose also from a coincidence between the performance and the battle of Verdun. The headline of *L'Oeuvre* ran: *We expected a steam-roller, we are given a Ballet Russe.*

The scandal of *Les Mariés* was a washing of dirty linen *en famille.* The audience fell into step. The

[1] With libretto by Cocteau, music by Satie, décor and costumes by Picasso, this ballet was presented in 1916. It was a flop (Tr.)

scandal arose from artists who considered the Eiffel Tower as their own property, the forefather of the machine and the first statement of modernism; they refused to see it put back among the charming bric-à-brac of the 1889 Exhibition.

*   *   *

Scandals about ideas do not concern me. I am only concerned with material scandals. If I am questioned about the scandal of a didactic play, I can give no answer. The scandal could occur in parliament, in church, in court, anywhere.

*   *   *

The absence of scandal in the case of *Le Boeuf sur le Toit*,[2] *Antigone, Roméo*[3] and *Orphée,* was the result of a long period when the snob, forewarned by his own mistakes, applauded himself.

MERCURE benefitted from this attitude on the part of the public. Moreover, the spectacle distracted them and prevented them from listening to Satie's orchestra.

On the eve of 1930 the snob, firmly on his hobby-horse again, permits himself to condemn, by silence, works in which Stravinsky gains the greatest victories over himself and over music.

[2] This 'farce' was first produced in 1920, with music by Darius Milhaud and décor by Raoul Dufy (Tr.)

[3] In 1926 Cocteau produced an adaptation of Shakespeare's *Romeo and Juliet.* (Tr.)

Since a ministerial visa is required for films, we are within a hair's breadth of censorship.

Censorship would be a terrible disaster for our times when youth is reclaiming lands left barren as a result of censorship. I do not prejudge the future. Censorship disarms a Proust, a Gide, a Radiguet, a Desbordes.[1] Think about it. Psychology is amputated. Authors lose their cases. Taxes, imprisonment, exile. The eternal scandal starts again.

*   *   *

The half-sleep of opium makes us pass down corridors and cross halls and push open doors and lose ourselves in a world where people startled out of their sleep are horribly afraid of us.

*   *   *

Opium may make us slightly visible to the invisible, may make spectres of us to frighten spectres in their own haunts.

Opium i........   ... every twenty

cases.

*   *   *

Never confuse the opium-smoker with the opium-eater. Quite different phenomena.

[1] Jean Desbordes published *J'Adore* in 1928. Cocteau led a campaign in support of the book, to which he wrote the preface. *Opium* is dedicated to Jean Desbordes (Tr.)

86

*   *   *

After smoking, the body thinks. It is not a question of the *confused thinking* of Descartes.

The body thinks, the body dreams, the body becomes soft and flaky, the body flies. The smoker embalmed alive.

*   *   *

The smoker has a bird's eye view of himself.

*   *   *

It is not I who become addicted, it is my body:
" . . . as certain chemical substances, essentially unstable when in their pure state, seize hold greedily of an element capable of giving them stability."

JULIEN BENDA.

My nature needs serenity. An evil force drives me towards scandal, like a somnambulist on the roof. The serenity of the drug used to protect me against this force which compels me to sit on the stool of repentance at a time when the mere reading of a newspaper would destroy me.

*   *   *

We only serve as a model for the portrait of our fame.

*   *   *

Everything is a question of speed (Immobile speed. Speed in itself. OPIUM: speed in silk). Beyond plants, whose speed is different from our own, revealing only a relative immobility, and the speed of metals, which show us an even greater relative immobility, lie other realms, whose speed is too slow or too fast for us even to see them or be seen by them. (LE CAP, the angel, the fan). It is not impossible that the cinema will one day be able to film the invisible and make it visible, adapting it to our rhythm as it adapts the gesticulation of flowers to our rhythm of life.

Opium, which changes our speeds, procures for us a very clear awareness of worlds which are superimposed on each other, which interpenetrate each other, but do not even suspect each other's existence.

*   *   *

"If Jesus, instead of having been crucified, had been stoned, what a change in the fortunes of Christianity."

Even if I go outside myself and adopt Benda's point of view, he is wrong. He forgets the strangeness of the naked Christ in churches and of a torture apparatus resembling the guillotine.

Christ, stoned, would provide a great image, erect, arms outstretched (Christ having become a cross), his face bleeding.

The dungeon: this gave birth to the mystery of

the vanished Christ. In churches: Christ carried off by the angels.

Christ beheaded: he dies by the sword (the cross). In churches: a sword in the form of a cross.

*   *   *

I do not condemn the music of words and all that it brings with it by way of dissonance, harshness and new sweetness. But a modelling of the soul attracts me much more. To oppose a living geometry to the decorative charm of the sentences. To have style and not *a* style. A style which does not allow itself to be imitated in any way. One would not know how to grasp it. A style which would only be born by cutting something from me, from a hardening of thought during its brutal passage from the interior to the exterior. With a bewildering halt like the bull as it comes into the ring. To expose our phantoms to the spray of a petrifying fountain, not to learn how to improve on ingenious objects, but to petrify, in passing, anything shapeless which comes out of us. To make concepts acquire volume.

Opium enables one to give form to the unformed; it prevents, alas, the communication of this privilege to anyone else. Even if it means losing sleep, I shall watch out for the unique moment in the process of cure when this faculty will still function a little and, inadvertently will coincide with the return of the power of communication.[1]

[1] LES ENFANTS TERRIBLES, born in 17 days with errors of style and spelling which I dare not touch.

Once a poet wakes up, he is stupid, I mean intelligent. "Where am I?", he asks, like ladies who have fainted. Notes written by a poet who is awake are not worth much. I offer them only for what they are worth, at my own risk. One more experience.

One must at all costs cure oneself of the tiresome habit of writing. Style coming from outside is unworthy, even if it superimposes itself exactly on to the interior style. The only possible style is the thought made flesh. Read official reports, the writing of mathematicians, surveyors, specialists in any branch whatsoever it may be. Suppress all other reading.

Anatole France: the classic according to the classics. Art according to art. Never was such a talent put into the service of platitude.

The lung is a sack of globules. Each globule is divided into alveoli which lead direct to the bronchi. One globule imitates the entire lung of a frog. The smooth internal surface is tapestried with a network of blood capillaries. In this way, if the lung were spread out, and ironed over, it would cover 200 square yards. You have read aright.

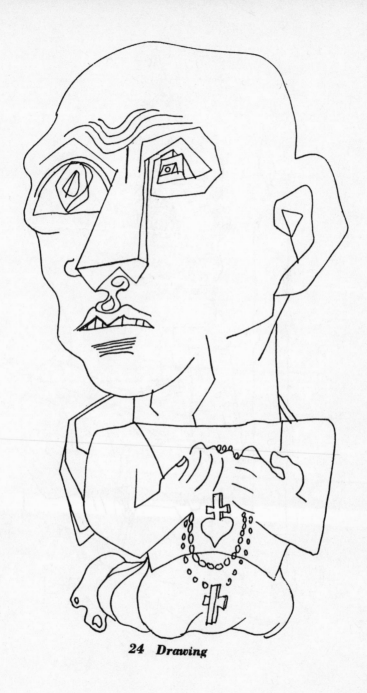

24 Drawing

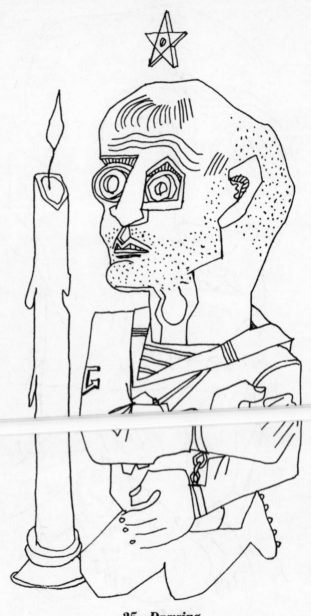

25 Drawing

26 Drawing

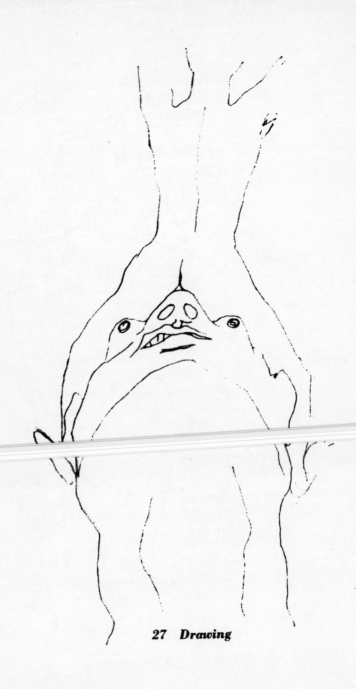

27 Drawing

Smoke, therefore, impregnates at one stroke 150 square yards of pulmonary surface.

The blood mass of the lung, which is only 7/1000ths of a millimeter thick, amounts to two pints.

Given the speed of pulmonary circulation, one can imagine the quantity of blood which passes through the respiratory apparatus.

Hence the instantaneous effects of opium on the smoker.

The smoker rises slowly like a balloon, turns again slowly and falls back on some dead moon whose weak pull prevents him from leaving.

Even if he gets up, talks, acts, is sociable, and appears to live, his gestures, gait, skin, looks, and words, do not reflect any the less a life subjected to other laws of paleness and gravity.

The return journey will take place at his own risk. The smoker first pays his ransom. Opium releases him, but the return is unattractive.

However, having returned to his planet, a nostalgia remains.

*   *   *

Death separates completely our heavy waters from our light waters. Opium separates them a little.

*   *   *

Opium is the only vegetable substance which

communicates the vegetable state to us. Through it, we get an idea of that other speed of plants.

*   *   *

One can say: the sun is big, this bit of dust is small, because they depend on our scale of values. It is foolish to say: God is big, an atom is small. It is very strange that hardly anyone lives with any feeling for the centuries which pass between each breath we take, of the worlds created and destroyed by our body, that the idea of our body's darkness conceals the fires which inhabit it, and that a difference in measurement renders incomprehensible the fact that these worlds may be civilised or dead; in brief, that the infinitely small may be a discovery instead of being an instinct.

It is the same for the infinitely big (big, but small by comparison with us), since we do not feel that our sky, our light, our space, constitute no more than a dark spot for the being whose body contains us and whose life (short for him) takes up centuries for us

wisdom of Moses was to confine men to their tiny houses.

*   *   *

THE NORMAL MAN: Elder pith addict, why live this existence? It would be better to throw yourself out of the window.

THE ADDICT: Impossible, I am floating.

THE NORMAL MAN: Your body will quickly reach the bottom.

THE ADDICT: I shall arrive slowly after it.

*   *   *

It is difficult to live without opium after having known it because it is difficult, after knowing opium, to take earth seriously. And unless one is a saint, it is difficult to live without taking earth seriously.

*   *   *

After the cure. The worst moment, the worst danger. Health with this void and an immense sadness. The doctors honestly hand you over to suicide.

*   *   *

Opium, which smooths out a little the tight folds which allow us to think we live a long time, by minutes, by episodes, first takes away our memory.

The return of memory and the feeling for time (even in my case where they barely exist in a normal state).

*   *   *

The spirit of the smoker moves without moving, like watered silk.

NOTES ON PROUST (THE RETURN OF MEMORY)

It is impossible for me to remember any first meeting with Proust. Our group has always treated him as a famous man. I see him, with a beard, seated on the red cushions at Larue's (1912). I see him, without a beard, at Madame Alphonse Daudet's, plagued by Jammes as by a gad-fly. I find him again, dead, with the beard he had at the start. I see him, with and without a beard, in that room of cork, dust and phials, either in bed, wearing gloves, or standing up in a washroom like a magistrate's office, buttoning a velvet waistcoat over a poor square torso which seemed to contain his mechanism, and eating noodles standing up.

I see him among the dust sheets. They lay over the chandelier and the armchairs. The naphthalene lit up the shadows. He stood erect against the chimney-piece in the drawing room of this *Nautilus* like a character out of Jules Verne, or else, near a picture hung with crepe, in a dresscoat, like Carnot dead.

Once announced by Céleste's voice on the telephone, he came to collect me at three in the afternoon so that I could go with him to the Louvre to see Mantegna's *St. Sebastian*. This canvas then occupied a place in the same room as *Madame Rivière, Olympia* and *Le Bain Turc*. Proust was like a lamp lit in broad daylight, the ringing of a telephone in an empty house.

Another time he was supposed to come (perhaps)

at about 11 o'clock at night. I was with my neighbour on the first floor, she of whom he wrote to me: 'When I was twenty she refused to love me; now that I am forty and have been the delight of the Duchesse de G . . . , must she refuse to read me?'

I had asked to be told. At midnight I went back upstairs. I found him on my landing. He was waiting for me, sitting on a seat in the darkness. 'Marcel,' I cried, 'why didn't you at least go in and wait for me? You know the door is left ajar.' 'Dear Jean,' he replied, in that voice that he used to muffle with his hand, the voice that was a moan, a laugh—'dear Jean, Napoléon had a man killed because he had waited for him in his room. Of course I would only have read Larousse, but there could have been letters and so on lying about.'

Alas, someone has stolen the book in which he used to write verses for me. I remember:

'Covering me with watered silk and sable,
Letting no ink from his big black eyes overflow,
Like a sylph on the ceiling, a ski on the snow,
Next to Nijinsky Jean leapt on the table.'

We were having supper after the theatre with the Russian ballet.

'It was in the crimson salon of Larue
Where the gold, of doubtful taste, was never rusty,
A doctor's beard, in thick and florid manner
Repeated: My presence may be incongruous to you

But if only one man remains I shall be he,
And my heart succumbed to the beats of *Indiana*.'

Was this doctor, who knew the exact terms, used
in the composition of Cottard? *Indiana* was the tune
of the moment.

At this time we used to send each other poetic
addresses. The Post Office did not get annoyed. For
instance:

Postman, bear these words, till they take their
    leave of you
At Boulevard Haussmann, Marcel Proust's, 102.
102, Boulevard Haussmann, all speed unloosed,
Run, postman, to Marcel Proust!

Proust replied with envelopes covered with a
spidery scrawl. In alexandrines he described the Rue
d'Anjou from the Boulevard Haussmann to the
Faubourg Saint-Honoré.

Near to the cave where Froment-Meurice flew one
    day,
Near to the ineffable Nadar . . .

I have forgotten the beginning and
out the end because flattery linked with reproaches
was his method of friendship.

I ask myself by what prodigies of love my dear
friends Antoine Bibesco, Lucien Daudet and Reyn-
aldo Hahn kept their balance. In spite of numerous
letters (there was one very fine one about the revival
of *Parade;* he compared the acrobats to the Dioscuri

and called the horse 'great swan with wild move-
ments') we stopped seeing each other as the result of
a ridiculous scene. I had gone to the Boulevard
Haussman like a neighbour, without hat and coat.
When I came in I said 'I've no coat, I'm frozen.'

He wanted to give me an emerald. I refused. Two
days later I had a cold. A tailor came to take my
measurements for a fur-lined coat. The emerald was
first of all intended to facilitate the purchase. I sent
the tailor away and Marcel Proust bore me a grudge
on this account. To his epistle of grievances he added
others, going on for twelve pages, which he charged
me to pass on to the Comte de B . . . This interminable indictment ended with a postscript: *In fact,
say nothing.*

*   *   *

I have recounted elsewhere (*Hommage à Marcel
Proust*, N.R.F.) the anecdote about the tip to the
concierge at the Ritz Hotel. 'Can you lend me fifty
francs?' 'Here you are, Monsieur Proust.' 'Keep it,
it's for you.'

Needless to say, the concierge was to receive three
times the amount next morning.

It is agreed that Marcel Proust did not write
romans à clef but certain of his friends supplied very
strong doses for his mixtures. He could not therefore
understand that the model, whose faults he depicted
as charm, would refuse to read his book, not out of
rancour, for the model was incapable of recognising

himself, but out of weakmindedness. He (Proust)
would then demand, with outbursts of childish
anger, something analogous to Fabre's huge success
with insects.

*   *   *

In order to understand the atmosphere at Proust's,
go to the Comédie Française. Push open the last door
on the right in a little corridor leading from the
stage to the big green room. It used to be Rachel's
dressing room. There, in an atmosphere as hot as a
furnace, you will see dust sheets, a harp, a painter's
easel, a harmonium, glass covers for clocks, bronzes,
ebony pedestals, empty glass cases, illustrious dust
. . . in short, you will be at Proust's, waiting for
Céleste to let you in.

I note this resemblance because of Rachel and
La Berma, because of everything that coincidence
arouses in us by way of sacred riddles.

*   *   *

depravity and condemns it because the senses are
responsible to the court of assizes. Genius is responsible to the court of miracles. Society lets genius live,
but does not take it seriously.

*   *   *

At the age when Christ began with death Alex-

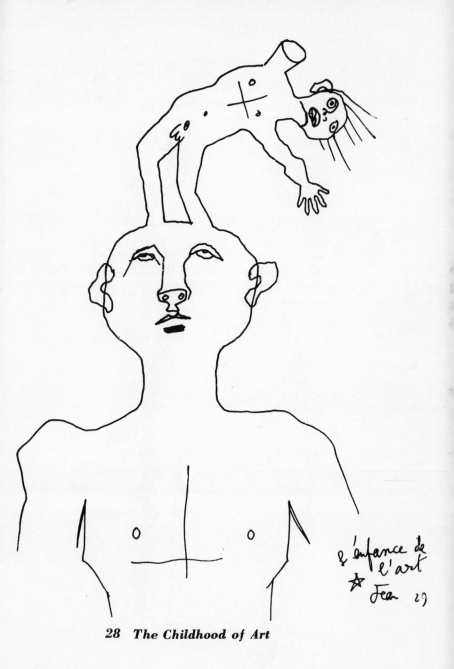

*l'enfance de
l'art
☆ Jean 29*

28   The Childhood of Art

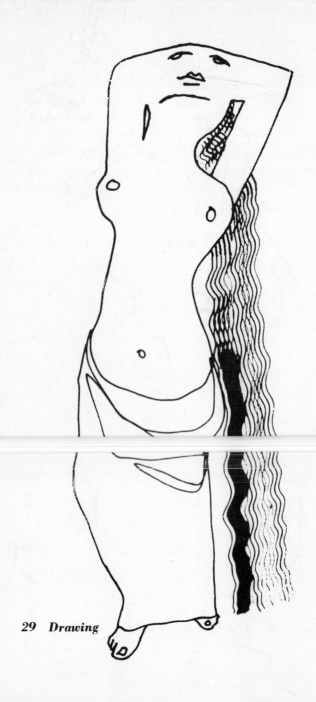

29 Drawing

ander died of a surfeit of glory. I imagine him, in despair, wondering sadly what he could still possess. One would like to reply: America, an aeroplane, a watch, a gramophone, the radio.

The embalmers stuff him with honey. He even had little bits of luck. His urine smelt of violets. One wonders if he is not a legend invented as an antidote to human disappointments. All that remains of his success is a profile on a coin which Barrès gave me. The other side bears a wise man, seated. Everyone knows that the two sides of a coin have little chance of ever meeting.

*   *   *

Christ and Napoleon are there. Impossible to get away from it. Happy fame with limited results; unhappy fame with unlimited results. According to Napoleon's system, a traitor loses the battle. According to Christ, a traitor wins the battle.

*   *   *

The aesthetics of failure are alone durable. He who does not understand failure is lost.

*   *   *

The importance of failure is capital. I do not speak of what fails. If one has not understood this secret, this aesthetic, this ethic of failure, one has understood nothing and fame is empty.

The number is never very numerous. It transforms cathedrals into chapels.

Admirers do not count. One must have utterly overwhelmed at least one soul. Make oneself loved through the gloomy indirectness of one's work.

*   *   *

'I've already done it.' *'That has already been done,'* stupid remarks; leitmotiv of the artistic world since 1912.

I detest originality. I avoid it as much as possible. An original idea must be used with the greatest precaution or one looks as though one is wearing a new suit.

*   *   *

A woman of seventy said to me 'People believe that the men of my generation, the members of the Jockey Club, were witty because of the number of wines drunk at table.'

After dinner everyone was a bit drunk. Some thought they were making mordant remarks, the others thought they were hearing them.

*   *   *

Opium lightens the mind. It never makes one

witty. It spreads the mind out. It does not gather it up into a point.

*　　　　　*　　　　　*

Le Grand Meaulnes. Le Diable au Corps. The good scholar Fournier; the poor scholar Radiguet. Those two short-sighted beings who barely emerged from death and very quickly returned to it again did not resemble each other, but their books convey the mystery of the childhood world, more unknown than the animal or vegetable world. Franz in class. Franz the wounded horseman, Franz in acrobat's tights, the somnambulist Augustin Meaulnes, the madwoman on the roof, Yvonne and Marthe destroyed by terrible children.

*　　　　　*　　　　　*

After the death of my grandfather, when I was ferretting about in his tempting room, a kind of scientific-artistic junk-shop, I found a full box of Nazir cigarettes and a cigarette-holder in cherry-wood. I pocketed the treasure.

In spring, I can see myself one morning at Maisons-Laffitte amid the tall grasses and the wild pinks, opening the box and smoking one of the cigarettes. The sensation of liberty, luxury and future was so strong that never again, whatever happens, shall I find anything akin to it. I could be proclaimed king, I could be guillotined, but the surprise and strangeness could not be more intense that that forbidden entry into the universe of grown-ups, universe of mourning and bitterness.

One more thing still delights me and takes me back instantaneously to childhood: thunder. Barely does it rumble, barely does a vast mauve flash of lightning follow than a softness, a feeling of relaxation overwhelms me. I detested the emptiness of our country house, the various people leaving (they were occupied outside) just as I detest anyone reading a newspaper in front of me. A thunderstorm assured a house full of people, a fire, games, a day that was intimate and without deserters. It is undoubtedly the old sensation of intimacy that governs the delight I feel when I listen to thunder.

*   *   *

CHILDHOOD

In 1915 our passion for adventures was responsible for the most comical of the Red Cross convoys. One night, at R . . , rain was falling in a farmyard. The

were full of seriously wounded Germans and their captured ambulance.

All at once, in a dark corner littered with ladders and ghosts I came across the following sight: Madame R's . . . young son, an eleven-year old boy scout, had hidden in an ambulance and followed us. Crouching there by the light of a lantern, armed with a pair of nail scissors, his tongue sticking out, his brow wrinkled, and too engrossed to see me, the boy was cutting the buttons off the uniform of a German officer who had had one leg amputated. Through half-closed eyes, like those of a statue, the officer watched the horrible rascal, who continued to collect his souvenirs as though he were gathering them from a tree.

*   *   *

Savonarola exploited this monstrous quality in children. His team of boy-scouts pillaged works of art, smashing them, tearing them down and dragging them to the purifying bonfire. The same children were to follow the preparations for his torture without missing a single detail.

*   *   *

I will not and cannot kill. Since I come of a hunting family it does happen, when I am in the country and a rabbit comes out of the undergrowth, that I take aim. I *wake up,* feeling stupid, alone with this gesture of death.

At V . . . I used to stride over crunching beet-roots, with a cocked rifle over my shoulder and the gamekeeper's son behind me. One day, outside a rabbit hole, I found the body of a baby rabbit. I came home rather proudly and exhibited it.

MY UNCLE: *You killed this animal?*

I (believing that truth was immediately known to

grown-ups, that truth was a grown-up in direct touch with my uncle, and that my uncle knew everything but would play the game with me): *Yes, uncle!*

MY UNCLE: *So you beat it to death with the butt?*

I (recognising the voice, still soft, and the look, already fierce, which heralded the usual end to the purge scene[1]): *I didn't kill it. It was dead when I found it.*

MY UNCLE: *Too late, my friend!*

They boxed my ears. They put me to bed. I could think things over and realise that truth is perhaps not on such intimate terms with grown-ups.

*   *   *

GETTING LUCK INTO A MUDDLE. In the evening, at Maisons-Laffitte, Uncle André used to send up balloons; but the wind had to drop first. At table my cousins and I would say: *If only the wind drops!* Then: *If only the wind doesn't drop* (thinking: *If only it does!*) Then: *If only it does!* (thus getting luck into a muddle). In this way a vacuum was

which certain details from a Van Houten cocoa poster played a subtle part. Next came such tricks that nowadays I would get lost among them, with or without opium.

A big conspiracy against luck: inviting people to four o'clock tea. 'This evening uncle will let off fireworks.' In the evening at 9 o'clock the gentlemen

[1] For details see *Portraits-Souvenir*, pages 51-54. *Paris Album*, page 41.

were smoking their pipes and the ladies were knitting in the garden. Uncle had forgotten his balloon. The bell rang. Families arrived, decked out with lace. Surprise. Shame. Excuses. The lace-clad families returned home. We were whipped. My cousin, a peculiar sort of crank who could only eat from plates decorated with Napoleon's monogram, shouted at the top of his voice: *Serves it right! Serves it right!* Served what right? Luck or truth, I no longer know.

*　　　*　　　*

My cousin carefully concealed the mechanism of a broken celluloid doll. When the spring was wound up tightly it was *the 'Moskovi'*; when the spring had run down it was *the 'Moskova'*. This ridiculous thing, which caused fits of giggling, sly looks and earnest discussions, greatly disturbed our families during the entire holidays, and they were spoilt for them.

*　　　*　　　*

I loved little B . . . I was two years younger. In order to marry her, I used to say, I'll wait until I'm two years older than she is. Little B . . . wanted to be pitied. She used to rub her gums with a dry toothbrush. Then, looking vague, she would cough, spit, and produce a red handkerchief. In dismay the whole family went to Switzerland. Her brothers exchanged Switzerland, which they disliked, for 'taws,' glass marbles with a twist of colour in the centre.

*   *   *

A mistress in a Moscow boarding-school said to the children: 'Keep order yourselves. Learn to pass judgment. If your friends behave badly, punish them.' Then she found a boy who had been hanged by the others. He was swaying right over the well of the staircase. The mistress did not dare untie him, cut the cord and send him crashing down.

*   *   *

Five of us in Form III at the Lycée Condorcet came from the Pension Duroc. The Pension replaced our families. In a single mottled green exercise book the Pension punished us, excused us and let us off detentions. This Pension did not exist. I had invented it out of nothing. When the trick had just been discovered I came home and pretended to have tummy-ache. It hurts there. It was my appendix. Appendicitis was all the rage. I allowed myself to be operated on in the rue Bizet because I had cold feet about school. I learned later that the headmaster wanted to let it pass, on the pretext that I was a credit to the drawing and gymnastics classes. I carried off the duffer's prizes; gymnastics and drawing.

*   *   *

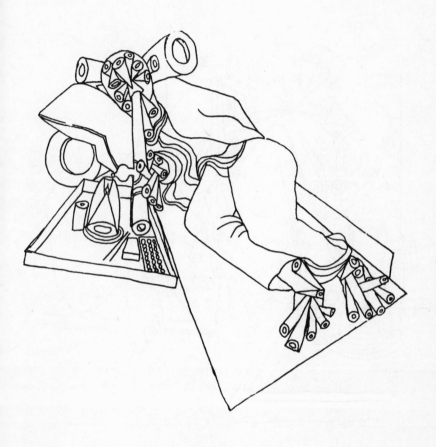

30   Drawing

31   Drawing

32   Drawing

33 *Drawing*

Through the wall my father and mother heard my brother Paul, when he was six years old, initiating a new German maid, who had arrived that morning: 'Ah, and then, you know, nobody ever washes me!'

Raymond Radiguet's brother came home from school, 28th out of 30. He told his father and added quickly, 'It's a lot!'

*   *   *

That is the essence of childhood. *Les Enfants Terribles* is about grown-up people, people of my type (the habit of living with people much younger than oneself). Articles and letters, including one very fine one from Professeur Allendy, informed me that the book was a book about childhood. I personally locate childhood further away, in a region that is more silly, more vague, more discouraging and more shadowy.

The 'game' would be more closely involved with it. That is why I hardly speak of it, and dare not go any deeper than our calculations with the Van Houten poster.

*   *   *

Raymond Roussel,[1] or genius in its pure state, inassimilable for the elite. *Locus Solus* questions the

[1] French surrealist writer, 1877-1933. (Tr.)

whole of literature and advises me once more to beware of admiration and to seek out love, which is mysteriously comprehending. In fact even one of the innumerable admirers of Anatole France or Pierre Loti cannot find one scrap of the genius which atones for their fame if he remains blind in front of *Locus Solus*. He therefore adopts France or Loti for the reason that separates us from them.

This proves, alas, that genius is a question of immediate dosage and slow evaporation.

*   *   *

Ever since 1910 I have heard people laugh about the 'rails of calf's lights' in *Impressions d'Afrique* Why should you imagine that the fear of being laughed at should affect Roussel? He is alone. If you should find him funny he will prove to you in a few lines (Olga Tcherwonenkoff) his feeling for what is comic set in tactful contrast to his gravely meticulous lyricism.

In a postscript to ~ ~ ~ ~ ~ ~ ~ ~ ~ ~ ~ ~ ~ ~ ~ ~ ~ ~ he wrote ~ ~ ~ ~ this passage from *Les Mariés de la Tour Eiffel*:

"First gramophone: But this telegram is dead.

Second gramophone: It's just because it's dead that everyone understands it."

This postscript proves that Roussel is not unaware either of what he is or of what is due to him.

*   *   *

Certain words make the public laugh. 'Calf's lights' prevent the delicate statue supported by these rails from being seen. In *Orphée* the word 'rubber' prevented Heurtebise's phrase 'She has forgotten her rubber gloves' from being heard. When I acted this part I succeeded, through imperceptible preparations, in reducing the laughter and finally in suppressing it. The audience were prepared without knowing it and expected the word 'rubber,' instead of being surprised by hearing it suddenly pronounced. Then they understood the surgical aspect of the term.

*   *   *

Roussel and Proust disprove the legend of the poet's indispensable poverty (his struggle for existence, garrets, and lobbying . . .). Rejection by the various elites and the automatic non-adoption of anything new cannot be explained only by the obstacles that a poor man overcomes gradually. A poor man of genius looks rich.

Thanks to his fortune Proust lived shut in with his world, he could afford the luxury of illness, and he was, in fact, ill because illness was possible; his nervous asthma and his ethic in the shape of fantastic care for his health brought on real illness and death.

Roussel's fortune allows him to live alone and ill without prostituting himself in any way. His riches protect him. He peoples emptiness. There is not the slightest grease-spot on his work It is a world suspended from elegance, fairyland and fear.

In the end *Impressions d'Afrique* leaves an impression of Africa. The story of the zouave is the only example of writing comparable to a certain type of painting which is sought by our friend Uhde, and he calls it painting *of the sacred heart*.

Apart from Picasso, in another medium, nobody has made better use of newspaper than Roussel. The judge's cap on Locus Solus's head, the plain round caps worn by Romeo and Juliet and Seil-Kor.

The same applies to the atmospheres in which Roussel's imagination moves. Old Casino decoration, old furniture, old costumes, scenes like those one sees painted on organs, and the fairground booths of prisons, the Decapitator and the Dupuytren Museum. The new is only presented in the shape of the fabulous: the seahorses and the Sauternes, Faustine, Rhedjed's flight, and Fogar's turn.

*   *   *

I have mentioned a similarity between Roussel

...... a social and physical similarity between silhouettes, voices and nervous habits acquired in the atmospheres where they both passed their youth. But the difference between their work is absolute. Proust saw a great number of people. He lived a most complex night life. He found the material for his great time-pieces outside. Roussel never sees anyone. He finds material only within himself. He even invents historical anecdotes. He operates his automatons without the slightest outside help.

*   *   *

Proust, Swann, Gilberte and Balbec always make me think of Souann in *Impressions d'Afrique,* the ancestor of Talou, and the phrase from *Locus Solus*: 'Gilbert waves over the ruins of Baalbek the famous uneven sistrum of the great poet Missir.'

Roussel's style is a means and not an end. It is a means which has become an end through the power of genius, for the beauty of his style arises from the fact that he applies himself to express difficult things in an accurate way, relying only on his own authority, and leaving no intriguing shadow round him. But since he is an enigma and has nothing round him, this illumination is much more intriguing.

If Giorgio de Chirico took to writing instead of painting I suppose he would create with his pen an atmosphere similar to that of the Place des Trophées.[1]

When we read the description of this square we think of him.

*   *   *

Under the influence of opium one delights in someone like Roussel and does not attempt to share this pleasure. Opium desocialises us and removes us

[1] (1930) *Hebdomeros* proves me right. Chirico has not read Roussel. There is a family likeness.

from the community. Further, the community takes its revenge. The persecution of opium addicts is an instinctive defence by society against an antisocial gesture. I regard these notes on Roussel as a proof of gradual return to a certain reduced communal life.

Instead of carrying these books away into my hide-out I would like to spread the knowledge of them. I had the opium-addict's laziness. One must beware of the downhill path to the communal grave.

It is to Gide, who generously read *Impressions d'Afrique* to us in the past, that I owe the discovery of *Locus Solus* and the recent reading of the admirable *Poussière de Soleils*.

*   *   *

Nobody knows how many solid walls, placed between the world and myself by opium, I had to overcome in order to help *J'Adore*.

Unless I had urgently wanted to emphasise the appearance of something truly magic I would never have made this effort. I would have carried the book off into the world where I live on my own.

*   *   *

In any case, should one intervene? Once again the question of American-style childbirth and medical progress. I think one should intervene to a certain extent. The principle of non-intervention could easily be an excuse for the heart's laziness.

In Roussel's eyes *the objects that he transfigures remain what they are*. It is the least artistic genius. It is the acme of art. Satie would say it was the triumph of the *amateur*.

Roussel's equilibrium is taken for disequilibrium. He hopes for official praise and he knows his work is misunderstood, thereby proving that official praise is not despicable because it is official but because it operates badly.

Raymond Roussel shows first of all the end without the means and he produces surprises which rest on a feeling of security (*Le Gala des Incomparables*). These means embellish the end of his book. But since they contain the strangeness that they owe to the author's person, they do not weaken the problems that they illuminate and to which they add a new and adventurous lustre.

The divinatory episodes which conclude *Locus Solus* are convincing. Here the author reveals first the experiments and then the devices behind them, but the devices depend on a reality, on Roussel, just as the devices admitted by the conjuror do not make us capable of performing the trick. The illusionist who reveals his device tranfers minds from a mystery they reject to a mystery they accept and places to his account approval which formerly enriched the unknown.

*   *   *

Genius is the farthest extreme of the practical.

*   *   *

Everything which logically and practically destines an ordinary object for an unforeseen use, before the slightest automatism or the slightest conscious memory have time to intervene, is genius.

*   *   *

In 1918 I rejected Roussel as likely to place me under a spell from which I could see no escape. Since then I have constructed defences. I can look at him from the outside.

..

'Any inflexibility of the mind will therefore be suspect to society because it is the sign of an activity which goes into isolation. And yet society cannot intervene here with any material repression since it is not materially affected. It is in the presence of a disturbing element . . . hardly a threat, at the most a gesture. It is therefore by means of a mere gesture

34   Drawing

35 *The Child Stealers*

that society will reply. Laughter should be something of this kind, a sort of social gesture.'

Bergson.

It is amusing and significant that Bergson never speaks of unjust laughter, official laughter in the face of beauty.

*   *   *

I have seen funny and splendid films, but I have only seen three great films: Buster Keaton's *Sherlock Holmes Junior,* Chaplin's *Gold Rush* and Eisenstein's *Battleship Potemkin.* The first is the perfect use of the marvellous, *The Gold Rush* is a masterpiece equal by its detail and ensemble to *The Idiot* and *The Princess of Clèves* and the Greek theatre and *Battleship Potemkin* where a country is expressed through one man.

As I re-read these notes (October, 1929) I add: Bunuel's *Chien Andalou.*

There it is, the style of the soul. Hollywood was becoming a luxury garage and its films were more and more beautiful types of motor-cars. With *Le Chien Andalou* we are back on our bicycles.

Go forward and fall, bicycle, bull-ring horse, flea-ridden donkeys, priests and Spanish dwarfs! Each time that blood flows in families or in the street they hide it, they put cloths over it, someone comes, people form a circle and prevent anyone from seeing. There is also the blood from the soul's body. It runs from horrible wounds, it runs from the corners of mouths, and the families, the policemen and the passers-by do not think of hiding it.

It is this inexpressible thing, this phantom of the awakening of condemned men, that the screen shows us like objects on a table.

Some Heinrich Heine is needed to relate the crimes of the little plump lady or the rôle in which Batcheff's heart stops beating several times in apartment houses in La Muette, in accursed Louis XVI bedrooms, in classrooms or in glades made for duelling.

One would like to know how to explain when Batcheff was standing in I don't know what (it was no longer a bedroom . . .), in despair? and that his mouth was set tight and that on the skin that set the mouth the young woman's armpit appeared and the young woman pulled and pulled and pulled at his tongue, and that she left him there and went out and banged the door, and that the wind ruffled his hair and his scarf, and that she screwed up her eyes, and that it was the seaside.

* *

Only Bunuel can bring his characters to those moments of paroxysm in suffering when it becomes natural and as though fated to see a man in a frock coat ploughing up a Louis XVI bedroom.

* * *

(1930) *L'Age d'Or,* the first masterpiece of the antiplastic. The only shadow of reproach: with Bunuel strength always appears to be accompanied by its conventional attributes.

But it's all the same! This is certainly the most exact study than can be made of the behaviour of man by a being who wishes to dominate us in the same way as we dominate the ants.

A revealing film. It is useless trying to agree about anything with people who are capable of laughing at the episode of the cow and the conductor of the orchestra.

*　　　*　　　*

Eisenstein's *Battleship Potemkin* illustrates that remark of Goethe's: the reverse of reality in order to obtain the maximum of truth.

For someone like Dreyer, Bunuel's technique must be mediocre, as though in 1912 a painter had demanded that Picasso should copy newspaper with a *trompe-l'oeil* effect instead of sticking it into his paintings.

*　　　*　　　*

If Bunuel fascinates Eisenstein this must be through Freud. The complex of hands and doors. His film must shock a Russian as being the height of individuality: an exhibited wound, Rousseau's buttocks, a police file or a form for a Wassermann test.

Bunuel could reply that *Battleship Potemkin* is a documentary film and provides a document about Eisenstein, since through his film the masses are incarnated in one single man who expresses the masses and expresses himself at the same time.

There is always documentation and every creative work is topical. It is impossible to avoid this. But it must be admitted that one of the numerous successful aspects of *Battleship Potemkin* is that it seems to have been filmed by nobody and acted by nobody.

*　　　　*　　　　*

(1930) I have come to know Eisenstein. I had seen aright. He invented the murder steps at the last moment. These steps become part of Russian history. Alexandre Dumas, Michelet and Eisenstein are the only true historians.

Tragic events acquire the power of those little obscene anecdotes, anonymous anecdotes which are perfected from one mouth to another and finish as

Marseilles stories.

*　　　　*　　　　*

Letter from the Columbia Recording Company. After my convalescence, if I record any poems, I will avoid having a photograph taken of my voice. Here is another problem. To solve it would open the door to astonishing possibilities of gramophone records becoming auditory objects instead of being mere photographs for the ear.

The improvised positioning of words, the vein of emotion, the chance meeting of serious words and a dance hall orchestra, a statue erected to chance, all in all a means of catching chance in a trap, of creating something definitive, a means which is absolutely new and absolutely impossible when one had to pay with one's person every evening.

Avoid poems in the style of *Plain-Chant*, choose poems from *Opéra*, the only ones which are hard enough to dispose of the human gesture, face and fluid in order to hold their own beside a black trumpet, saxophone or drum.

*   *   *

Speak quietly very close to the microphone, rest the microphone against one's neck. I suppose in this way any pleasant voice would be better than Chaliapine or Caruso.

*   *   *

Make re-recordings. Changes of speed which have become normal again. Celestial voices.

*   *   *

The important thing is that the voice should not

resemble my voice but that the machine should use a clean, new, hard and unknown voice manufactured in collaboration with the machine. *Le Buste,* for example, declaimed or pronounced by a machine as it might have been through an antique mask by antiquity.

*   *   *

One should not worship machines any longer or use them as workmen. One should collaborate with them.

*   *   *

The Dutch sea captain Vosterloch discovered in Tierra del Fuego natives of a bluish colour who corresponded by means of sponges capable of retaining "the sound of the spoken voice."

"With the result that when they wish to ask for something or to speak from a distance they speak into one of these sponges then they send them to their friends who, having received them, press them softly and make words come out of them like water and through this admirable method they know all that their friends desire."

Courrier Véritable (April 1632).

One thinks of the plant which retained pictures discovered by Fogar deep down in the water. (*Impressions d'Afrique*).

With what pleasure would one applaud Stravinsky on the cheeks of one's neighbours.

*   *   *

If you are surprised that a person reveals himself to be superior to what he should be as the result of his education, upbringing, background and friends, there is a possibility that he is an opium-addict.

*   *   *

They spend their time making me sweat day and night. Opium takes its revenge. It does not like its secrets to be sweated out.

*   *   *

Sentence from a dream. Let this box of sweets jump the queue . . .

*   *   *

This morning the birds are jubilant. I had forgotten the morning and the birds.
Tweet, tweet, tweet!
Tweet, tweet, tweet!
Tweet, tweet, tweet! the trinket in the cages,
Tweet, tweet, tweet! the traps among the bushes,
Tweet, tweet, tweet! the curls upon the scissors,
Tweet, tweet, tweet! a circuit of swallows,

Tweet, tweet, tweet! a figure eight with wings,
Tweet, tweet, tweet! so the birds sing.

The boy at the Hôtel de la Poste in Montargis
who was graciously brought along by the birds (tweet,
tweet, tweet! the salt-cellars. Tweet, tweet, tweet!
watering between the green boxes with spindle-trees
on the pavement, tweet, tweet, tweet!) knew how to
fly, without the slightest play on words and without
the slightest equipment.

The proprietor's wife: "Anselme, fly a bit to show
Monsieur Cocteau."

I am noting word for word the transparent absur-
dities of morning drowsiness.

*   *   *

Last night I had my first long dream in colour, the
first since my cure which had contours and a general
atmosphere. When I was suffering from opium-
poisoning I remember a ghost of the alkaline of
dreams, the framework that it filled. Today I remember almost the entire dream inhabited with precise
~~~~~~~~ ~~~~ ~~~~~ ~~~~~~ with very plausible
dialogues, and with women whom I do not know, or
whom I ought to know. They included Mary Garden.

Concerning an itinerary and a film based on *The
Devil in the Flesh.* This dream borrowed an episode
not from reality but from another old dream which
I remembered having dreamt at the moment when I
dreamt of the episode. Therefore I took my dream
for a reality foretold by a dream.

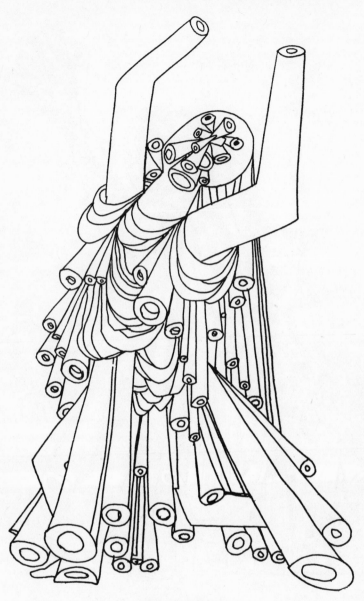

36   Drawing

Oreste

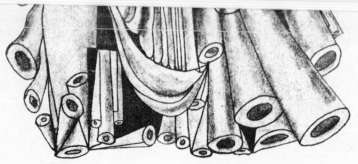

37 Orestes

38 Drawing

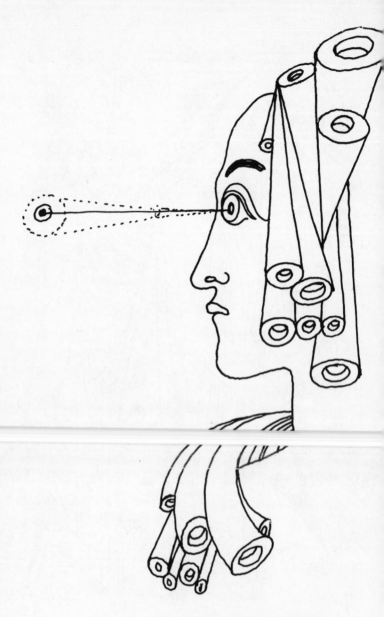

39   The Dreadful Children

*　　　　*　　　　*

The episodes in dreams, instead of dissolving on some nocturnal screen and evaporating quickly, make deep veins like agate on the confused surfaces of our bodies. There is a type of education through dreams. This education is superimposed on any other. It may be said of a person who has been educated forever by dreams that he has studied the inhumanities thoroughly. All the more so because the classic dreams, the first dreams that come to one as a child, far from being naive, are like the Atridae and feed on tragedy.

*　　　　*　　　　*

Gags in American films. Editing films. Dreams, instead of putting their atrocious gags on the screen, edit the film and leave it to us. Afterwards their gags can be useful for editing other films.

*　　　　*　　　　*

The living language of dreams. The dead language of waking . . . We must interpret and translate.

*　　　　*　　　　*

I must ask the disciples of Freud for the meaning of a dream I have often had ever since I was 10 years old, several times a week. This dream stopped in 1912.

My father, who was dead, was dead no longer. He had become a parrot in the Pré-Catelan, one of those parrots whose chatter remains always associated for me with the taste of frothing milk. During this time my mother and I would go and sit at a table at the Pré-Catelan farm in which several farms were mixed up with the cockatoo terrace in the Zoo. I knew that my mother knew, and did not know that I knew, and I guessed that she was looking to see which one of the birds my father had become and why he had become a bird. I would wake up in tears because of her face as she tried to smile.

*　　　　　*　　　　　*

Young people from foreign countries often write to poets asking to be excused for reading them so badly and knowing our language so badly. It is I who should be forgiven for writing a language instead of

*　　　　　*　　　　　*

A scandal in Rome—*Trésors de Pie et vols d'oiseaux*. Still more children snatched by angels.—Angels who steal children.—Poets take advantage of angels.—Birds are accused of being too light.—Leonardo and Paolo di Dono bear witness to this.

*   *   *

Only a bird could allow himself to paint *The Profanation of the Host*. Only a bird was pure enough, selfish enough and cruel enough.

*   *   *

A letter from Corot: "This morning I took extreme pleasure in seeing again a small picture of mine. There was nothing in it but it was charming and looked as though it had been painted by a bird."

*   *   *

Guillaume Apollinaire, who was wounded when he had a post with the Colonial Office, wrote to me from a drawing-room full of fetishes a letter which ended like this:

> We'll talk of Europe or Asia,
> We'll talk about your projects,
> And as the kings of poetry
> We'll talk of the gods, our subjects.

Over the top he added a streamer with this device: "The bird sings with its fingers."[1]
And this passage from *Locus Solus*:

"A wisp of smoke from the sleeper's brain showed, as in a dream, eleven young men bending

[1] Cocteau used this phrase in his film *Orphée*. (Tr.)

half over under the influence of fear inspired by a certain airy, almost diaphanous ball which seemed to form the objective for the dominating upward flight of a white dove and cast on the ground a faint shadow that enveloped a dead bird."

*　　　　　*　　　　　*

SOUVENIR OF THE MAS DE FOURQUES. The peacock closes his fan with a Spanish gesture. With his cruel glance, his enamelled face, his dog collar, his emerald-studded corsage and his aigrette he leaves the theatre. His court train carries away the astonished eyes of the crowd. Leaning forward on the edge of the stone staircase he calls conceitedly for his chauffeur.

*　　　　　*　　　　　*

HE WHO PAYS HIS DEBTS. In this thankless age I should like to write a book of thankfulness. Among other advances Gide made to me was the one where-by he reformed my handwriting. With the stupidity of extreme youth I had devised a type of handwriting for myself. This false handwriting, which a graphologist would have found revealing, falsified me down to my very soul. I added a small loop on to the big loops of my capital J's. One day as he was leaving my house Gide said to me at the door, overcoming his embarrassment, 'I advise you to simplify your J's.'

---

[1] I know sculptures by Giacometti which are so solid and light that they look like snow retaining the foot prints of a bird.

I was beginning to understand what miserable fame is built up on youth and brio. This loop operation saved me. I forced myself to go back to my real handwriting and with the help of handwriting I rediscovered the naturalness I had lost.

*   *   *

Beware of your handwriting, complete your letters, join them together and do not write t's which can be mistaken for d's.

The height of inelegance: an illegible signature.

One day, when I was writing an address at Picasso's house, he looked at me and said with a strange smile: "Oh! you too?" I was in the process of joining together the letters in the name that I had just written. Picasso knows everything: naturally he knew that too.

*   *   *

A writer develops the muscles of his mind. This training leaves hardly any leisure for sport. It demands suffering, falls, laziness, weakness, setbacks, exhaustion, mourning, insomnia, exercises which are the reverse of those which develop the body.

*   *   *

The success of the devil among intellectuals is a mistake. God and simple folk! Now, without the devil, God would never have reached the public at large.

A poet could reproach God about this as a concession.

*   *   *

A propos studies dealing with the dialects of primitive peoples, I like to imagine a translation of Proust into a primitive tongue where one word would signify the jealousy *which consists of* . . . or the jealousy *which consists of* . . . We would have pages reduced to one line and SWE, for example, would signify DU COTE DE CHEZ SWANN.

*   *   *

I have found that the system of not receiving newspaper cuttings and relying on chance alone to put us in contact with important articles leads us to be very impolite. But since there is not a shadow of politeness in the articles which count and since their writers

speak (whom they treat, what is more, as though he were dead), our impoliteness deprives us only of superficial articles and never of serious studies.

*   *   *

The inexplicable importance of poetry. Poetry considered as algebra.

128

First of all, poetry only solicits the toughest minds, minds which should scorn it as a luxury; the worst of all.

If it were proved to me that I would condemn myself to death if I did not burn L'ANGE HEURTEBISE,[1] I would perhaps burn it.

If it were proved to me that I would condemn myself to death if I did not add to or take away one syllable from the poem, I could not change it, I would refuse, I would die.

When I see all the artists who used to make a practice of despising the fashionable world because they had not as yet been received into it, lapse into snobbishness after the age of forty, I congratulate myself on having had the possibility of going into the fashionable world at sixteen and on having had enough of it by the time I was twenty-five.

*   *   *

In favour of opium. Opium is anti-social. Except in the case of active and overwhelmingly healthy people, opium removes all trace of sociability.

I remember exactly (I was not yet taking opium) the evening when I decided I would go out no more and when I had the proof that fashionable artists are coming down in the world.

It was at the British Embassy. The Ambassadress was giving a reception for the Prince of Wales.

The poor prince, red in the face, wearing uniform

[1] A poem which Cocteau first published in 1925. (Tr.)

and boots, was hopping like a bear from one leg to the other, fingering his leather straps, lowering his head, alone under a chandelier in the centre of a large pool of gleaming parquet. The group of guests stood crowding up to a certain invisible line while the people who were introduced crossed the polished area beyond. The ladies curtsied and came back; very few men were presented.

Suddenly, the Ambassador, Lord D . . . , came up, took hold of me by the scruff of the neck and dragged me off more dead than alive and threw me to the prince like a bone to a dog, saying: "Here's someone who'll amuse you."

I admit that answers come to me slowly. Usually I discover my answers too late and I kick myself for it. This time, the reply reaction functioned marvellously. The prince looked at me overwhelmed with embarrassment. I ASKED HIM QUESTIONS. This was certainly the first time that anyone had asked him questions. He replied with an astonished expression, as meek as a lamb.

The next day Reginald Bridgeman, Lord D . . .'s private secretary, who was to become a socialist leader, told me that the entire Embassy was wondering why I had asked the prince questions. "Explain to them," I told him, "that after the Ambassador's rudeness the only thing left for me to do was to ask the prince questions, to make him understand that he was with an equal."[1] (The prince must have

[1] A man.

thought later that I had played the fool in order to justify the Ambassador's remark).

From that day I wrote letters asking for my name to be removed from the invitation lists and threw my dress coat on to the rubbish heap.

*   *   *

X . . refuses a decoration. What is the point of refusing it if the work accepts it? The only thing one can be proud of is of having worked in such a way that an official reward for your labour cannot be envisaged by anyone.

Many surprising fashions in dress have arisen from the fact that a famous man or woman tried to conceal some infirmity.

*   *   *

The anonymous letter is an epistolary genre. I have only received one and it was signed.

In 1929 artists and magazines are discovering those photographs taken upside down and the wrong way round which delighted and helped us in 1914.

*   *   *

Posters, shop-windows and luxury publications are using on a big scale everything which, in 1916, caused the untidiness of a room like mine in the Rue d'Anjou to be fabulous. I did not notice it. I read the articles about the room with surprise. I found this untidiness heartbreaking and normal.

It is odd to see how a small group of people who believed that they set the style still imagine that periods lead to something. "Ah," says the snob of 1929, "at last it's possible to photograph some old planks and write underneath 'New York,' or a gaslamp and write underneath 'Nude study,' or put side by side a chinese torture and a game of football. At last we've got there. It was not without difficulty. Long live the studio!" They fail to understand that these private entertainments are reaching the wide public and others are being prepared in secret.

*   *   *

Legend gathers round poets who live in glass houses. If they hide and live in some unknown cellar, the public thinks: "You're hiding, you want us to believe there is something where there is nothing."

On the other hand, if they look at the glass house, the public thinks: Your oversimple gestures conceal something. You are deceiving us, you are mystifying

search, find, symbolise, and mystify.

People who come close to me and fathom the mystery, pity me and become angry; they do not know the advantages of a ridiculous legend: when they throw me to the flames they burn a lay figure who is not even like me. A bad reputation should be maintained with more love and more luxury than a little dancer.

In this way, I can explain the fine phrase that Max Jacob wrote to me: *One should not be known for what one does.*

Fame in one's lifetime should only be used for one thing: to allow our work, after our death, to start out with a name.

*   *   *

Because I authorised Louis Moysès, who deserves every help, to take the titles of my works as fetiches for his sign-boards, people believe that I run bars where my habits and my health do not even allow me to go any longer. I visited LE GRAND ECART one morning and I only know LES ENFANTS TERRIBLES from photographs. This does not prevent the night-birds from recognising me there or the police from noting in their files: owner of LE BOEUF SUR LE TOIT, occasional poet (sic). *Douce France!* And to think that abroad I would be flattered, housed and over-whelmed. My laziness would be regarded as an aristo-cratic style: ungrateful France prefers my patriotism. It is true that Paris is one of the few capitals where they do not yet try to suppress nicotine. One of my friends used to live in Berlin at the Adlon. In the evening, in the restaurant, a delightful person asked him for a light.

Do you live at the Adlon?

Yes, how do you know?

I am the hotel liftman.

At that moment, my friend added, I saw nothing

but emptiness. That is the result of a country which suppresses nicotine. There remained nothing before my table, neither man nor woman nor prostitute, nor liftman—just emptiness.

We shall soon have genius removed from art and considered as nicotine. It is almost the case in Russia where the last resource of someone like Eisenstein will be to explain all his film discoveries as dreams. "It was a dream!"—"It was only a dream!" and therefore an inoffensive type of individualism.

I have lived each period of my life so passionately and blindly that I have completely forgotten one of them. An object or a person which typified it leaps into my memory without any anchor. Where did he come from? Where did she come from? I search. I do not find. The background has disappeared.

I do not speak of the great actors or of the great settings for the drama.

*   *   *

TESTE IS NOT VALERY

island which I have inhabited ever since I was born and which I cannot leave now.

Sometimes he reaches the shore and wanders about, trying to overcome the deadly sleep that emanates from the outer trees. It is the moment, after dinner, when Madame Teste watches him move away, still seated, leaving in the armchair only a great empty smoking mass.

If I, a man from the centre, were to venture out, I would be able to see him a long way off leaning up against a tree, resembling his column in the Opera House. But it frightens me to leave the middle of the island and then, what is the use of it? With his pride, he would never stoop to questioning the natives. What is more, I speak a different language. Further, I do not know this island well. I am used to it. I put up with it. I need a report from a tourist, from a Teste, and a Teste does not penetrate into it.

(October 1929)

*   *   *

GRATUITOUS DEEDS

Lafcadio believes he kills without provocation. Now he throws out of the door the things he has always thrown out of the window, the type that his type drives away and cannot admit under pain of death.

When Lafcadio disposes of F . . . , it is as if he were looking at himself in the railway carriage window, squeezing the sides of his nose between his finger-nails and making the dead fat come out of it. I think of him after this hygienic, coquettish action (the murder), sitting down again, tapping himself, and flicking the dust off the revers of his new suit (1930).

*   *   *

Opium has broad shoulders. After my cure I begin to experience once again the sufferings that I blamed it for and which it mitigated; I remember the same sufferings tortured me in the past, when I did not know opium (1930).

*   *   *

One day, I was going to the rue Henner, passing the rue La Bruyère, where I spent my youth at number 45, a house where my grand-parents lived on the first floor while we lived on the mezzanine floor (the ground floor, consisting of store rooms and the hall, included only a study looking on to the courtyard and the trees of the Jardin Pleyel). I decided to overcome the anguish which usually made me run along this street like a man both deaf and blind. Since the main gates of number 45 were half open, I went in under the archway. I looked with surprise at the trees in the courtyard where I used to spend the summer bicycling and decorating Punch and Judy shows, when a suspicious *concierge,* appear-

closed in the past, asked me what I was doing there. When I replied that I had come to have a look at the house of my childhood, she said: "You do surprise me," left the window, came through the hall to join me, inspected me, refused to be convinced by any proof, threw me out and banged the main gates, giving rise, with this sound of distant cannon fire, to a host of new memories.

After this setback, I thought of going along the street from the Rue Blanche to number 45, closing my eyes and letting my right hand trail along the houses and the lamp-posts as I always used to do when I came back from school. The experience did not yield very much and I realised that at that time I was small and that now my hand was placed higher and no longer encountered the same shapes. I began the manoeuvre again.

Thanks to a mere difference of level, and through a phenomenon similar to that whereby a needle rubs against the grooves of a gramophone record, I obtained the music of memory and I discovered everything again: my cape, my leather satchel, the name of the friend who accompanied me, and the name of our teacher, some precise phrases I had said, the marbled cover of my note-book, the timbre of my grand-father's voice, the smell of his beard and the material of the dresses worn by my sister and mother, who were At Home on Tuesdays.

*　　　　　*　　　　　*

I wonder how people can write the lives of poets since the poets themselves could not write their own life. There are too many mysteries, too many true falsehoods, too many complications.

What can be said of the passionate friendships which must be confused with love, and yet nevertheless are something else, of the limits of love and friendship, of this region of the heart in which unknown senses participate, which cannot be understood by those who live standard lives?

Dates overlap, years mingle together. The snow melts, the feet fly away; no footprints remain.

*   *   *

To some extent space plays the same role as time. It already gives perspective. A foreigner who judges our character from our work judges us better than our entourage, who judge our work from ourselves.

*   *   *

I dream that it should be granted to me to write an *Oedipus and the Sphinx*, a sort of tragi-comic prologue to *Oedipus Rex*, preceded in its turn by a broad farce with soldiers, a ghost, the producer and a woman spectator.

The performance would go from farce to the depth of tragedy, interspersed with my gramophone records and a tableau vivant *The Marriage of Oedipus and Jocasta* or *Plague at Thebes*.

*   *   *

SIX WEEKS AFTER WEANING

For a week I have looked well again and the strength has come back to my legs (Jouhandeau has pointed out one thing that is true: my hands still look ill). Now, I find that for a week I have not been

40   Drawing

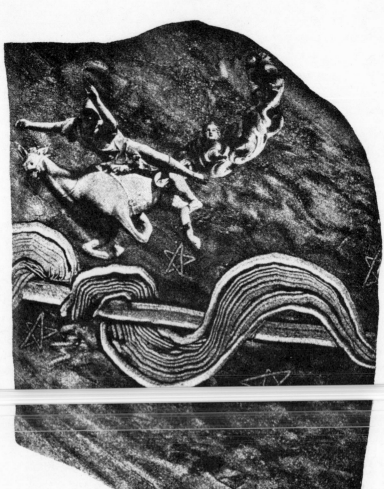

41   *I leave Saint-Cloud*

La révolte des
équipages

Jean
A
1929

42 The Crews' mutiny

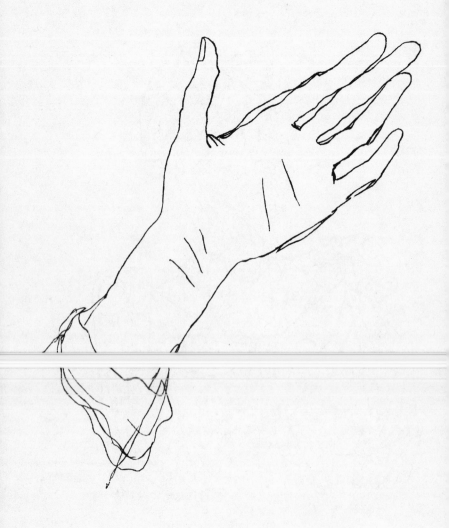

43 The bird charmer's destiny

able to write any more about opium, I do not need to any more. The opium problem is receding. I would have to invent something.

I was therefore eliminating through ink, and even after the official elimination there was an unofficial elimination with a flow which became solid through my desire to write and draw. I allowed these drawings or notes only the value of frankness, and they seemed to me to be a derivative, a discipline for the nerves, but they became the faithful graph of the last stage. Sweat and bile precede some phantom substance which would have dissolved, leaving no other trace behind except a deep depression, if a fountain pen had not given it a direction, relief and shape.

Waiting for a period of calm to write these notes was trying to relive a state which is inconceivable as soon as the organism is no longer in it. Since I have never granted the slightest importance to the setting and since I was using opium as a remedy, I was not unhappy at seeing my state disappear. Whatever one renounces is a dead letter for those who imagine that the setting plays a part . . . I hope that this reportage finds a place among doctors' pamphlets and the literature of opium; may it serve as a guide to the novices who do not recognise, beneath the slowness of opium, one of the most dangerous faces of speed.

*   *   *

First ride in a car. I went to read *La Voix Humaine* to the reading committee of the Comédie Française.

A small dark room full of pictures representing Racine and Molière and Rachel. A green carpet. A courtroom lamp. The *Sociétaires* listened, taking up the poses of some famous pictures: "Z . . . reading X . . ." The administrator sat opposite me. Behind him, a Burgrave with a white beard.

'Why are you letting the Comédie Française have a play?' I am continuously asked this question. It is ridiculous. Apart from the fact that the Comédie Française is a theatre like any other, better kept than any other, with the advantage of a gilded setting and a public more greedy for sentiment than sensation, its stage remains the only one where a one-act play can be put on.

The boulevard theatre has changed places. It is now in the so-called *avant-garde* theatre. The public look for exciting audacity and success prevents the directors from introducing variety and trying works out there.

The old *avant-garde* theatre has been replaced by cinema studios, which dethrone the former boulevard theatre. The dramatists who survive f . . . . are trying to rejuvenate their formulae.

In short, since the young theatres are full up and their public expect everything except something new, which, putting fashion out of fashion, does not seem to be fashionable, and since Paris does not like the system which in Germany consists of giving an hour of theatre after the theatre, there is only the Comédie Française which can put on these short plays in the middle of the performance. The other theatres are forced by custom to sacrifice them as curtain raisers.

*   *   *

Death of the theatre through the talking films, therefore the renaissance of the true theatre.

This theatre, which seemed too strange and too exceptional to exist, will alone survive because nothing can take its place. Every pure form is irreplaceable. The shapes, colours and the wonder of human flesh, the mixture of the true and the false are all irreplaceable.

The boulevard theatre will become the talking film made perfect. Where can one place the one-act play, the rapid, lively, concise one-act play, save at the Comédie-Française, which preserves the remains of an age when fêtes and royal ballets permitted a short spectacle?

The one-act play will find its place again between a classic Chaplin film and a talking film. This type of programme, which will include further the best music-hall turns, will be the origin of the future Comédie-Française. I advise this theatre to be in a district capable of furnishing a basic audience, a local audience which could be joined later by the audience of snobs and amateurs, that is Montparnasse. Let me add that it should be simple, in the red and gold style, with model lighting systems and young scene-shifters who are worth all the lifts and revolving stages in the world.

141

*   *   *

My childhood: the red Jules Verne books with their gilt edges, Robert Houdin, busts, wax models and roundabouts.

The Comédie-Française. The busts, the balustrades, the girandoles, the velvet, the draperies, the footlights: wonderful! a fiery sword separating the imaginary world from our world, and the solemn curtain which should only rise on scenes of murder, historical groups from the Musée Grévin, the cruel farces of Molière and the fatality of the Atrides.

La Voix Humaine is an ugly one-acter, an entry of appearance against the aesthetes, the snobs and the young (the worst snobs), capable of moving only those who expect nothing and who have no prejudices.

Making other people say: "It's not Cocteau. Why did he write that? So and so could do it just as well and even better, because he's cleverer." Finding again the true public, which one only finds at the Comédie-Française and at Bobino. Big box-off

.....ices. It is not the public which one must shock, but the elite; one must obtain a scandal of the commonplace, go into the repertory, have a long run. The mistake, in 1930, would be to achieve a scandal similar to *Parade* in 1917 and take the play off.

*   *   *

The people who mistake a landscape by Corot for a landscape by Harpignies should be made to say 'it's like Bataille!'

*   *   *

Perhaps the idea of having only one character on the stage came from my childhood. I used to see my mother, wearing a décolleté dress, leave for the Comédie-Française. Mounet-Sully performed *La Grève des Forgerons* after *L'Enigme* by Hervieu. He acted this monologue surrounded by extras consisting of the Sociétaires dressed as judges, members of the jury, and policemen. I used to dream about this theatre and I did not suspect that, with its gilt and its spectacle, it was so close to Guignol. I wondered how a single actor could act a play.

*   *   *

The principle of novelty becomes very difficult to recognise when our age forces us to remove from it its usual attributes of strangeness.

*   *   *

Just as it is easy to put oneself on an equal footing with the public through a somewhat unpleasant turnabout, so it is difficult to reach the point when the curve of our work brings us to that ideal point of contact where the Shakespeares and the Charlie Chaplins always work.

We can begin to see what will make 1930 look ridiculous. Just as 1900 remains the period of poker-work, the 'modern-style,' the Palais de Glace, the slow waltz and the cake-walk, 1930 will be the period of contrasts, contrasts in the Hugo or Balzac style, including montage films, and their master-piece, *La Melodie du Monde,* which will remain supremely typical. All these contrasting ideas come from the contrasts of shapes, the cube and the sphere.

I am incapable of writing a play and putting it on for or against something; but I congratulate myself that an instinct of revolt, a spirit of contradiction which dwells within the poet, prompted me to write a play of unity, a static play, a complete contradiction to the syncopation of contemporary jazz and cinema.

*　　　　　*　　　　　*

My next work will be a film.

*　　　　　*　　　　　*

April 1930. I wanted to reply to the critics and profit from the genuine absense of bitterness, to lean on the success of a work made for success. Tristan Bernard telephones me: "Buy *Le Journal.*" On the first page he replies in my place, he spares me this lack of taste.

"A play like Jean Cocteau's one-acter *La Voix Humaine* has greatly frightened our good critics. And yet they were docile, on the whole well disposed to follow the author in the direction in which they expected him to go. Then, suddenly, the author proves them wrong. His simple and profound one-act play reveals a truth that no one expected, a truth to which no one was accustomed, a virgin truth. The experts stood still before the disconcerting brilliance of this golden coin of a play which did not seem to be valid currency because it had not been in circulation long enough."

*   *   *

Douce France. Playwrights receive money from the Société des Auteurs in accordance with the number of acts in the play.

I was entering *La Voix Humaine*:

The typist: Comédie-Française . . . How many acts?

Myself: Only one. I'm sorry about it.

The typist: It gets you a foot inside the door.

*   *   *

Les Enfants Terribles was written under the obsession of *Make Believe* from *Show Boat*; those who like this book should buy the record and read the book while playing it.

Now that I am cured, I feel empty, poor, heart-broken and ill. I float. The day after to-morrow I leave the clinic. Where should I go? Three weeks ago, I felt a sort of pleasure. I was asking M . . . questions about altitude and about little hotels in the snow. I was going to come out.

But it was a book that was going to come out. A book is coming out, is going to come out, as the publishers say. It is not I. I could die . . . the book does not care. The same game always begins again and every time one allows oneself to be taken in.

It was difficult to foresee a book written in seventeen days. I had the illusion that it was a question of myself.

The work which exploits me needed opium; it needed me to leave opium; once more, I will be taken in. And I was wondering, shall I take opium or not? It is useless to put on a carefree air, dear poet. I will take it if my work wants me to.

And if opium wants me to.

Dargelos' snow-ball was a very hard snow-ball.

Now I have so often read, and people have so often said to me: "This ball contained a stone" that I doubt it. Love gives second sight. Would Gérard have guessed correctly?

I did not know that the book began with a white ball, ended with a black ball, and that Dargelos sent both of them. The premeditated look of instinctive equilibrium.

People who think that they like *Les Enfants Terribles* often say to me 'except the last pages.' Now the last pages wrote themselves first, one night in my head.

I no longer breathed, I did not move, I did not make notes. I was torn between the fear of losing them and the fear of having to write a book which would be worthy of them.

*   *   *

The poem which helped me to get started after the gift of the last pages.

THE COMRADE[1]

This marble punch was a snowball,
And it starred his heart
And it starred the victor's jacket,
Starred the black victor whom nothing protects.

Stupefied he stood
Barelegged in the lair of solitude,

[1] *The Comrade* has been recorded on one side of a Columbia record. It is also found in the film *La vie d'un poète* which was begun in April and finished in September 1930.

Beneath the gilded walnuts, mistletoe and holly,
Starred over like the blackboard in the classroom.

Often this begins at school,
These punches that fill the mouth with blood
These hard snowball punches,
That beauty jabs at the heart in passing by.

Saint-Cloud, February, 1929.
Notes of 1929 and 1930.Roquebrune.

BIBLIOGRAPHY OF WORKS
BY JEAN COCTEAU

━━━━━━━━━━━━━━*)))))))))))))(((((((((((*━━━━━━━━━━━━━━

Established by Louis Bonalumi for publication with
LES OEUVRES COMPLETES DE JEAN COCTEAU (Lausanne:
Marguerat; 1946—50).

I. POESIE

LA LAMPE D'ALADIN: 1909. Société d'Editions, Paris.

LE PRINCE FRIVOLE: 1910. Mercure de France, Paris.

LA DANSE DE SOPHOCLE: 1912. Mercure de France, Paris.

LE CAP DE BONNE ESPERANCE: 1919 Editions de la Sirène, Paris.

L'ODE A PICASSO: 1919. François Bernouard, Paris.

POESIES: 1919. Editions de la Sirène, Paris.

ESCALES: 1920. (En collaboration avec André Lhote). Editions de la Sirène, Paris.

VOCABULAIRE: 1922. Editions de la Sirène, Paris.

LA MORT DE GUILLAUME APPOLLINAIRE: 1923. "Vient de paraître" revue, Paris.

PLAIN-CHANT: 1923. Stock, Paris.

LA ROSE DE FRANCOIS: 1924. François Bernouard, Paris.

POESIES (1916—1923): 1924. (Le Cap de Bonne Espérance—Ode à Picasso—Poésies—Vocabulaire—Plain-Chant—Discours du Grand Sommeil 1916—1918, INEDIT). Editions de la Nouvelle Revue Française, Paris.

CRI ECRIT: 1925. (Frontispice de Henri de la Jouguière). Imprimerie de Montane, Montpellier.

PRIERE MUTILEE: 1925. Editions des Cahiers Libres, Paris.

L'ANGE HEURTEBISE: 1925. (Avec une photo de l'ange, par Man Ray). Stock, Paris.

OPERA: (1925—1927): 1927. (Couverture de Christian Bérard). Stock, Paris.

MORCEAUX CHOISIS, POEMES: 1932. Libraire Gallimard, Paris.

MYTHOLOGIE: 1934. (En collaboration avec Giorgio de Chirico). Editions des Quatre Chemins, Paris.

ENIGME: 1939. (Gravure d'après un dessin de l'auteur). Editions des Réverbères, Paris.

ALLEGORIES: 1941. Librairie Gallimard, Paris.

JEAN COCTEAU: 1945. Choix de poèmes par H. Parisot, avec une étude de R. Lannes. Pierre Seghers, Paris.

LEONE: 1945. Illustré par l'auteur. Librairie Gallimard, Paris.

LEONE: 1945. Avec deux lithographies de l'auteur. Librairie Gallimard, Paris.

POEMES: 1945. (extraits de: Le Cap de Bonne Espérance — Discours du Grand Sommeil — Poésies — Ode à Picasso—Vocabulaire—Plain-Chant — Opéra — Musée secret). Keaser, Editions du Grand Chêne, Lausanne.

LA CRUCIFIXION: 1946. Paul Morihien, Paris.

POESIES: 1947. Palimurge, Paris.

POEMES: 1948. (Léone—Allégories—La Crucifixion

ANTHOLOGIE POETIQUE: 1951. (Le Cap de Bonne Espérance—Discours du Grand Sommeil—Poésies—Vocabulaire — Plain-Chant — Opéra — Léone — Allégories — La Crucifixion—Neiges—Un ami dort—Le Rythme grec, inédit—Atalante court à sa perte, inédit, couverture et illustrations de l'auteur). Club Français du Livre, Paris.

JEAN COCTEAU: 1952. Choix de poèmes par H. Parisot et R. Lannes. Nouvelle édition refondue et complétée. (Poèmes manuscrits inédits). Pierre Seghers, Paris.

LE CHIFFRE SEPT: 1952. *Avec une lithographie de l'auteur.* Pierre Seghers, Paris.

LA NAPPE DU CATALAN: 1952. *64 poèmes et 16 lithographies en couleurs de Jean Cocteau et Georges.* Imprimerie Feguet et Baudier, Paris.

OPERA: 1952. *Illustré par l'auteur.* Arcanes. Editions du Rocher, Monaco.

DENTELLE D'ETERNITE: 1953. Poème-objet. Pierre Seghers, Paris.

APPOGIATURES: 1953. *Avec un portrait de l'auteur par Modigliani et un dessin de Hans Bellmer.* Editions du Rocher, Monaco.

VERSAILLES: 1953. La Table Ronde, no. 68, Paris.

CLAIR OBSCUR: 1954. Editions du Rocher, Monaco.

II. POESIE DE ROMAN

LE POTOMAK (1913—1914): 1919. Précédé d'un Prospectus (1916) et suivi des Eugènes de la Guerre (1915). Société Littéraire de France, Paris.

LE GRAND ECART: 1923. Illustration de l'auteur. Librairie Stock, Paris.

THOMAS L'IMPOSTEUR: 1923. Edition de la Nouvelle Revue Française, Paris.

LE POTOMAK (1913—1914): 1924. Précédé d'un Prospectus (1916). Texte définitif. Librairie Stock, Paris.

THOMAS L'IMPOSTEUR: 1927. Illustrations de l'auteur. Edition de la Nouvelle Revue Française, Paris.

LE LIVRE BLANC: 1928. Edition des Quatre Chemins, Paris.

LES ENFANTS TERRIBLES: 1929. Bernard Grasset, Paris.

LE LIVRE BLANC: 1930. Illustrations de l'auteur. Editions du Signe, Paris.

LES ENFANTS TERRIBLES: 1931. 32 bois originaux de L. Dollian. Arthème Fayard et Cie, Paris.

LE FANTOME DE MARSEILLE: 1933. Tirage à part de la Nouvelle Revue Française, Paris.

LES ENFANTS TERRIBLES: 1939. Librairie Flammarion, Paris.

LA FIN DU POTOMAK: 1939. Librairie Gallimard, Paris.

DEUX TRAVESTIS: 1947. (Le fantôme de Marseille—Le numéro Barbette). Illustrations de l'auteur. Fournier, Paris.

LES ENFANTS TERRIBLES: 1948. Illustrations de l'auteur. Editions du Frêne, Bruxelles.

LES ENFANTS TERRIBLES: 1950. Illustré par Nancy Gräffe. Richard Masse, Paris.

LES ENFANTS TERRIBLES: 1951. Club Français du Livre, Paris.

LE LIVRE BLANC: 1953. Illustrations de l'auteur. Paul Morihien, Paris.

III. POESIE DE THEATRE

PARADE: 1919. (Ballet réaliste. Décors de Picasso, musique d'Erik Satie. Rome, 1916. Théâtre du Châtelet, Paris, 1917). Rouard Lerolle, Paris.

LE BOEUF SUR LE TOIT ou "The Nothing-Doing Bar": 1920. (Farce. Décors et cartonnages de Raoul Dufy, musique de Darius Milhaud. Comédie des Champs-Elysées, Paris, 29 février 1920—Coliseum, Londres, 12 juillet 1929). La Sirène Musicale, Paris.

LE GENDARME INCOMPRIS: 1921. (Critique bouffe, en

roulenc). Editions de la Galerie Simon, Paris.

LES MARIES DE LA TOUR EIFFEL: 1923. (en collaboration avec les musiciens du "Groupe des six." Décors d'Irène Lagut, Costumes de Jean Hugo. Théâtre des Champs-Elysées, Paris, 18 juin 1921). "Les Oeuvres Libres" Fayard, Paris.

LES MARIES DE LA TOUR EIFFEL: 1924. (en collaboration avec les musiciens du "Groupe des six." Décors d'Irène Lagut, Costumes de Jean Hugo. Théâtre des Champs-Elysées, Paris, 18 juin 1921). *Avec un portrait de l'auteur par J.- V. Hugo.* Editions de la N.R.F., Paris.

LES BICHES: 1924. (Ballet en 1 acte, en collaboration avec Darius Milhaud. Théâtre de Monte-Carlo, 6 janvier 1924). *Avec un portrait de Mme Nijinska par J. Cocteau.* Editions des Quatre Chemins, Paris.

LES FACHEUX: 1924. (Ballet en 1 act, en collaboration avec Louis Laloy et Georges Auric. Théâtre de Monte-Carlo, 19 janvier 1924). *Avec un portrait de G. Auric par Jean Cocteau.* Editions des Quatre Chemins, Paris.

ROMEO ET JULIETTE: 1926. (Prétexte à mise-en-scène d'après le drame de W. Shakespeare. 5 actes et 23 tableaux. Décors mobiles et costumes de Jean Hugo, musique de scène d'après des airs populaires anglais arrangés et instrumentés par Roger Desormières. Théâtre de la Cigale, Paris, 2 juin 1924). *Avec bois de Jean Hugo.* Au Sans Pareil, Paris.

ORPHEE: 1929. (Tragédie en 1 acte et un intervalle. Théâtre des Arts, Paris, 17 juin 1926). Stock, Paris.

OEDIPE ROI—ROMEO ET JULIETTE: 1928. (Oedipe Roi—adaptation libre d'après Sophocle. Nouveau Théâtre Antoine, Paris. juin 1937). *Frontispices de l'auteur.* Librairie Plon, Paris.

ANTIGONE—LES MARIES DE LA TOUR EIFFEL: 1928. (Antigone, d'après Sophocle. Décors de Picasso, musique de A. Honegger. Théâtre de l'Atelier, Paris, 20 décembre 1922). Librairie Gallimard, Paris.

OEDIPUS REX: 1928. Opéra-oratorio en deux actes, d'après Sophocle. Musique de Stravinsky. Texte de J. Cocteau mis en latin par J. Daniélou. Iière exécution en concert au Théâtre de Sarah-Bernhardt, 1927. Iière représentation au Kroll-Oper, Berlin, le 25 février 1928.

ANTIGONE: 1928. (Tragédie lyrique en 3 actes, musique de A. Honnegger, Paroles de Paul Collaër, suivie des principaux extraits de la presse française et étrangère concernant la création au Théâtre Royal de la Monnaie de Bruxelles et au Stadttheater d'Essen). Editions Maurice Sénart, Paris.

LA VOIX HUMAINE: 1930. (Pièce en 1 acte, créé par Mlle Berthe Bovy. Théâtre de la Comédie Française, Paris, 17 février 1930. Décor de Christian Bérard). *Avec un dessin de C. Bérard*. Stock, Paris.

LA MACHINE INFERNALE: 1934. (Pièce en 4 actes, Décors et costumes de Christian Bérard. Théâtre Louis Jouvet (Comédie des Champs-Elysées), Paris, 10 avril 1934). *Illustré par l'auteur*. Bernard Grasset, Paris.

L'ECOLE DES VEUVES: 1936. (D'après le conte de Pétrone, *La Matrone d'Éphèse*. 1 acte écrit pour Mlle Arletty). Représenté à l'A.B.C., Paris.

LES CHEVALIERS DE LA TABLE RONDE: 1937. (Pièce en 3 actes. Décors et mise-en-scène de l'auteur. Théâtre de l'Oeuvre, Paris, 14 octobre 1937). Librairie Gallimard, Paris.

LES PARENTS TERRIBLES: 1938. (Pièce en trois actes. Théâtre des Ambassadeurs, Paris, 14 novembre 1938). Librairie Gallimard, Paris.

LES MONSTRES SACRES: 1940. (Portrait d'une pièce en 3 actes. Décors de Christian Bérard. Théâtre Michel, Paris, 17 février 1940). *Illustrations par Christian Bérard*. Librairie Gallimard, Paris.

LE BEL INDIFFERENT: 1940. (Ecrit pour Mlle Edith Piaf. Décor de Christian Bérard. Théâtre des Bouffes Parisiens, Paris.

LA MACHINE A ECRIRE: 1941. (Pièce en 2 actes, décors de

Librairie Gallimard, Paris.

RENAUD ET ARMIDE: 1943. (Tragédie en 3 actes, en vers. Décors et costumes de Christian Bérard. Théâtre Français, Paris, avril 1943). *Illustrations de l'auteur*. Rombaldi, Paris.

ORPHEE: 1944. *Lithographies de l'auteur*. Rombaldi, Paris.

RENAUD ET ARMIDE: 1945. *Lithographies de Christian Bérard*. Librairie Gallimard, Paris.

L'AIGLE A DEUX TETES: 1946. (Pièce en 3 actes. Théâtre Hébertot, Paris, novembre 1946). Librairie Gallimard, Paris.

LE JEUNE HOMME ET LA MORT: 1946. (Ballet sur la Passacaille en lit mineur de J. S. Bach, créé par Jean Babilée et Nathalie Philippart). Opéra de Paris.

THEATRE de Jean Cocteau: 1948. (T. I: Antigone—Les Mariés de la Tour Eiffel—Les Chevaliers de la Table Ronde—Les Parents Terribles. T. II: Les Monstres Sacrés—La Machine à Ecrire—Renaud et Armide—L'Aigle à Deux Têtes). Librairie Gallimard, Paris.

THEATRE DE POCHE: 1949. (Parade—Le Boeuf sur le Toit—Le Pauvre Matelot—L'Ecole des Veuves—Le Bel Indifférent—Le Fantôme de Marseille—Anna la Bonne—La Dame de Monte Carlo—Le Fils de l'Air—Le Menteur—Par la Fenêtre—Je l'ai Perdue—Lis ton Journal—La Farce du Château). *14 dessins de l'auteur.* Morihien, Paris.

Adaptation d'UN TRAMWAY NOMME DESIR: de Tennessee Williams, d'après la traduction de Paule de Beaumont: 1949. Couverture et lithographies de Jean Cocteau. (Théâtre Edouard VII, Paris, 17 octobre 1949). Bordas, Paris.

PHEDRE: 1950. (Tragédie chorégraphique, musique de Georges Auric, décor et costumes de l'auteur, chorégraphie de Serge Lifar. Opéra de Paris, 1950). L'Opéra de Paris, no. 1, juillet 1950.

BACCHUS: 1952. (Pièce en 3 actes, Théâtre Marigny, Paris 20 décembre 1951). Librairie Gallimard, Paris.

THEATRE DE POCHE: 1953. (14 dessins de l'auteur). Editions du Rocher, Monaco.

LA DAME A LA LICORNE: 1953. (Ballet en un acte, légende, décor et costumes de Jean Cocteau, arrangements musicaux de J. Chailley. Gärtner Théâtre, Munich, 9 mai 1953).

LA MACHINE INFERNALE: 1954. "Paris-Théâtre," no. 81, février. Paris.

IV. POESIE CRITIQUE

LE COQ ET L'ARLEQUIN: 1918. (Notes autour de la musique) avec un portrait de l'auteur et deux monogrammes par P. Picasso. Editions de la Sirène, Paris.

PREFACE à *Le bal du Comte d'Orgel par Raymond Radiguet*: 1920. Bernard Grasset, Paris.

CARTE BLANCHE: 1920. (Articles parus dans *Paris-Midi* du 31 mars au 11 avril 1919). Editions de la Sirène, Paris.

LA NOCE MASSACREE: 1921. Souvenirs 1. Visites à Maurice Barrès. Editions de la Sirène, Paris.

LE SECRET PROFESSIONNEL: 1922. Stock, collection "Les Contemporains," Paris.

PICASSO: 1923. Stock, collection "Les Contemporains," Paris.

D'UN ORDRE CONSIDERE COMME UNE ANARCHIE. (Allocution prononcée au Collège de France le 3 mai 1923).

AUTOUR DE THOMAS L'IMPOSTEUR: 1923. Publié dans les Nouvelles Littéraires du 27 octobre 1923, Paris.

FERAT: 1924. Edizioni dei Valori Plastici, Rome.

LA JEUNESSE ET LE SCANDALE (conférence faite le 27 février 1925).

LE SECRET PROFESSIONNEL: 1925. *Suivi des Monologues de l'Oiseleur* et augmenté de 12 *dessins en couleurs de l'auteur. Au Sans Pareil, Paris.*

LE RAPPEL A L'ORDRE: 1926. (Le Coq et l'Arlequin—Carte-Blanche—Visites à Barrès—Le Secret Professionnel—D'un ordre considéré comme une anarchie—Autour de Thomas l'Imposteur—Picasso. 1918—19). Stock, Paris.

LETTRE PLAINTE: 1926. R. Sacier, Paris.

LETTRE A JACQUES MARITAIN: 1926. Avec réponse de Jacques Maritain à Jean Cocteau. Stock, Paris.

AUTOUR D'ORPHEE ET D'OEDIPE: (Conférence faite le 7 décembre 1927).

PREFACE à *Les Jeunes Visiteurs* par Daisy Ashford: 1927. Mermod, Lausanne.

PREFACE à *J'adore* par Jean Desbordes: 1928. Bernard Grasset, Paris.

LE NUMERO BARBETTE: 1928. (Avec Antigone et Les Mariés de la Tour Eiffel). Librairie Gallimard, Paris.

PREFACE à *La passion et la mort de Jeanne d'Arc* par Pierre Bost: 1928. "Le cinéma romanesque," no. 7, Librairie Gallimard, Paris.

LE MYSTERE LAIC: 1928. Essai d'étude indirecte, *avec 5 lithographies de G. de Chirico.* Editions des Quatre Chemins, Paris.

QUELQUES LIGNES: 1928. Montpellier.

UNE ENTREVUE SUR LA CRITIQUE AVEC MAURICE ROUZAUD: 1929. "Les amis d'Edouard" no. 145, Paris.

PREFACE à *Mon amant se marie* par Thora Dardel: 1930. M. P. Trémois, Paris.

OPIUM. Journal d'une désintoxication: 1930. *Dessins de l'auteur.* Stock, Paris.

PREFACE à *Alexandre* par Klaus Mann: 1931. Stock, Paris.

ESSAI DE CRITIQUE INDIRECTE: 1932. (Le mystère laïc— Des beaux-arts considérés comme un assassinat). Bernard Grasset, Paris.

PORTRAITS-SOUVENIR: 1935. *Illustré par l'auteur.* Bernard Grasset, Paris.

MON PREMIER VOYAGE: (Tour du monde en 80 jours): 1937. Librairie Gallimard, Paris.

PREFACE à *Paris le jour* (60 photographies de Schall): 1937. Editions Arts et Métiers Graphiques, Paris.

PREFACE à *La vie de la danse* par Julie Sazonova: 1937. Denoël, Paris.

UNE INTERVIEW SUR LA POESIE. M. P. Lagarde interroge Jean Cocteau: 1938. Conferencia, No. XXLL—1er novembre, Paris.

NOTES de Jean Cocteau pour *Ballets russes de Diaghilev* (1909—19) exposition organisée par Serge Lifar: 1939. Édition J. de Brunhoff, Paris.

25ème ANNIVERSAIRE DE LA MORT D'UN POETE. GUILLAUME APOLLINAIRE: 1943. COMOEDIA, no. 123, 6 novembre. Paris.

PREFACE à *The Princess of Clèves* by Madame de la Fayette: 1943. London: The Nonesuch Press.

SERGE LIFAR A L'OPERA défini par Paul Valéry, parlé par Jean Cocteau, vécu par Serge Lifar: 1943. Editions de Champrosay, Paris.

LE GRECO (avec un sonnet de Gongora traduit par Jean Cocteau): 1943. Au Divan, Paris.

PREFACE à *Mes nouvelles chansons* par Charles Trenet. Avec un dessin de Jean Cocteau: 1943. Editions Salabert.

PRESENTATION de l'exposition *Jodelot* à la Galerie Charpentier: 1944. Paris, 76, Faubourg St. Honoré.

PORTRAIT DE MOUNET-SULLY: 1945. Avec 16 dessins de l'auteur. François Bernouard, Paris.

LE RIRE: 1945. Texte et dessins de Jean Cocteau. "Pan, artistique, satirique et littéraire," Paris.

DE LA FRIVOLITE: 1946. Dossiers No. 2, J. B. Janin, Paris.

DE LA MUSIQUE ENCORE ET TOUJOURS: 1946. Recueil ~~collectif. T~~ ~~Éditions du Tambourinaire, Paris.~~

PREFACE à *Edouard Bourdet et ses amis* par Denise Bourdet: 1946. La jeune Parque, Paris.

PREFACE à *Bach-Yen ou la fille au coeur fidèle* par Tran Van Tung: 1946. J. Susse, Paris.

PREFACE à *Louis Cappiello, sa vie, son oeuvre* par J. Viénot: 1946. Editions de Clermont, Paris.

HOMMAGE A MOLIERE. Texte lu pour l'inauguration de la Salle du Luxembourg, le 20 novembre 1946, par M. J. Bertheau.

HOMMAGE A RACINE. Texte dit pour l'anniversaire de Racine, à la Comédie-Française, le 21 novembre 1946, par M. Denis d'Inès.

LA BELLE ET LA BETE: 1946. Journal d'un film. J. B. Janin, Paris.

LETTRE DU 15 JUIN 1945 SUR L'ECRITURE ET LA VIE EPISTOLAIRE: 1947. 69, Quai d'Orsay, Paris.

LES OMBRES HEUREUSES DE MONTE CARLO. Textes de J. Cocteau, eaux-fortes en couleurs de Claude Lepape: 1947. Paris.

PREFACE à *La machine à courage*. Souvenirs de Georgette Leblanc: 1947. J. B. Janin, Paris.

LE FOYER DES ARTISTES: 1947. Librairie Plon, Paris.

LA DIFFICULTE D'ETRE: 1947. Morihien, Paris.

DEUX TRAVESTIS: 1947. *Le Fantôme de Marseille—Le numéro Barbette. Illustrations de l'auteur.* Fournier, Paris.

PREFACE à *Histoire du Chevalier Desgrieux et de Manon Lescaut* par l'Abbé Prévost: 1948. Stock, Paris.

PRESENTATION d'*Anna Karénine* par Léon Tolstoï: 1948. Bordas, Paris.

PREFACE à *L'Empereur de Chine* par Jean-Pierre Aumont: 1948. Nagel, Paris (Collection "Théâtre contemporain").

MAURICE BARRES: 1948. La Table Ronde, Paris no. 11, Novembre.

REINES DE FRANCE: 1948. Bernard Grasset, Paris.

PRESENTATION DE *Almanach du théâtre et du cinéma*: 1949. Editions de Flore, Paris.

PRESENTATION de *Swing* par Gaston Criel: 1949. E.U.F., Paris.

PREFACE à *Choix de lettres de Max Jacob à Jean Cocteau, 1919—1944*: 1949. Morihien, Paris.

PREFACE à *La bonne planète* par Charles Trenet: 1949. Brunier, Paris.

IGOR STRAVINSKY: 1949. (Articles de J. Cocteau, etc.)
A Merle Armitage book, edited by Edwin Corle, Duell,
Sloan & Pearce, New York.

LOUXOR: 1949. La Table Ronde, no. 22.

DUFY: 1949. Flammarion, Paris (collection "Les Maîtres
du dessin").

LETTRES AUX AMERICANS: 1949. Bernard Grasset, Paris.

PREFACE à *Paris tel qu'on l'aime* par Doré Ogrizek: 1949.
Editions ODE, "Le Monde en couleurs," Paris.

MAALESH: 1949. Journal d'une tournée de théâtre.
Librairie Gallimard, Paris.

INEDITS, ETUDES, DOCUMENTS: 1950. "Ecran du Monde."
Bruxelles.

NOTICE SUR CHRISTIAN BERARD in *Christian Bérard* par
Gabrielle Vienne: 1950. Editions des Musées Nation-
aux, Paris.

ORSON WELLES, en collaboration avec André Bazin.
Portrait par J. Cocteau: 1950. Chavano, Paris (collection "Le cinéma en marche").

MODIGLIANI: 1950. Hazan, Paris.

ENTRETIENS AUTOUR DU CINEMATOGRAPHE: 1951. (Recueillis
par André Fraigneau). Editions A. Bonne, Paris.

JEAN MARAIS: 1951. Dessin de l'auteur. Calmann Lévy,
Paris.

15 mars 1951.

PREFACE à *Mes quatre cent coups* par Roland Toutain:
1951. Amiot-Dumont, Paris.

PRESENTATION de *Le Château de Canelfour* par Odette
Joyeux (Paris, Théâtre des Mathurins, 6 décembre
1950): 1951. Librairie Gallimard, Paris.

TEXTE de Jean Cocteau en *Centro Internazionale delle
arti e del costume*: 1951. Imprimerie De Bertieri.

PREFACE à *Le Coffret hindou* par Out el Koulem: 1951.
Librairie Gallimard, Paris.

PREFACE à *Nicole's Guide in Paris*: 1951. Amiot-Dumont, Paris.

DE L'INNOCENCE CRIMINELLE: 1952. La Table Ronde, Paris (no. 11).

JOURNAL D'UN INCONNU: 1952. Bernard Grasset. Paris.

JEAN LURCAT: 1952. Maison de la Pensée Française, Paris.

PRESENTATION de *Lettres imaginaires* par Max Jacob: 1952. Les amis de Max Jacob, Paris.

PREFACE à *Le Roman de Renart*: 1952. Lithographies de J. Cocteau. Les Editions des Arceaux, Montpellier.

DIALOGUE AVEC JEAN COCTEAU in *Cinéma oeil ouvert sur le monde*: 1952. La Guilde du Livre, Lausanne.

PRESTIGE DES MILLE ET UNE NUITS: 1953. Editions de la Bibliothèque.

PRESTIGE DE LA DANSE avec Serge Lifar et Gisèle d'Assailly 1953. 15 photos et 6 dessins. Editions Ch. Portal, Paris.

PREFACE à *Poésie pour tous* par C. Day Lewis et Y. Peres: 1953. Pierre Seghers, Paris.

LA DIFFICULTE D'ETRE: 1953. Editions du Rocher, Monaco.

PABLO PICASSO: 1953. La Table Ronde, Paris (no. 9).

LETTRE-PREFACE à *Feux vifs et flammes mortes pour un astre éteint* par Michel Beaugency: 1953. Presses du Livre Français Paris.

PREFACE à *Italie* par Gino Spaventa Filippi: 1953. Nagel, Paris-Genève.

PREFACE à *La Grèce*: 1953. "Le monde en couleurs" ODE, Paris.

PREFACE à *L'Allemagne*: 1954. "Le monde en couleurs" ODE, Paris.

PROMENADES AVEC GUILLAUME APOLLINAIRE: 1954. Le flâneur des deux rives, no. 2, juin. Paris.

DEMARCHE D'UN POETE. Illustré par l'auteur. 1954. S.A.B.R.I.

LA CORRIDA DU IER MAI: 1955. Bernard Grasset, Paris.

DISCOURS D'OXFORD: 1956. Librairie Gallimard. Paris.

DISCOURS DE RECEPTION A L'ACADEMIE FRANCAISE et
REPONSE D'ANDRE MAUROIS: 1956. Librairie Gallimard,
Paris.

V. POESIE GRAPHIQUE

DESSINS: 1923. Stock, Paris.

LE MYSTERE DE JEAN L'OISELEUR Monologues: 1925.
Edouard Champion, Paris.

MAISON DE SANTE: 1926. Briant Robert, Paris.

POESIE PLASTIQUE—OBJETS—DESSINS: 1928. Editions des
Quatre Chemins, Paris.

VINGT-CINQ DESSINS D'UN DORMEUR: 1929. Mermod.
Genève.

SOIXANTE DESSINS POUR LES ENFANTS TERRIBLES: 1934.
Bernard Grasset, Paris.

DESSINS EN MARGE DU TEXTE DES CHEVALIERS DE LA TABLE
RONDE: 1941. Librairie Gallimard, Paris.

DROLE DE MENAGE: 1948. Morihien, Paris.

DROLE DE MENAGE: 1952. Editions du Rocher, Monaco.

VI. POESIE CINEMATOGRAPHIQUE

LE SANG D'UN POETE: 1932. Film de Jean Cocteau,
musique de Georges Auric.

LE BARON FANTOME: 1943. Film de Serge de Poligny.

L'ETERNEL RETOUR: 1944. Film de Jean Delannoy,
scénario et dialogues de Jean Cocteau. Musique de
Georges Auric.

LA BELLE ET LA BETE d'après le conte de Mme Leprince
de Beaumont: 1945. Film, adaptation et dialogues de
Jean Cocteau.

L'ETERNEL RETOUR: 1946. Scénario Collection "Roman-
film."

RUY BLAS: 1947. Film en collaboration avec Pierre
Billon. Adaptation et dialogues de Jean Cocteau.

RUY BLAS: 1947. Texte de l'adaptation. Morihien, Paris.

LA VOIX HUMAINE: 1947. Film. En collaboration avec Rossellini.

L'ETERNEL RETOUR: 1947. Scénario. 21 photographies et un portrait de l'auteur par Laure Albin Guillot. Nouvelles Editions Françaises, Paris.

LE SANG D'UN POETE: 1948. Scénario illustré de 50 photographies de Sacha Masour. Robert Marin, Paris.

LES PARENTS TERRIBLES: 1948. Film. Scénario, dialogues et réalisation de J. Cocteau.

L'AIGLE A DEUX TETES: 1948. Film. Scénario, dialogues et réalisation de J. Cocteau.

L'AIGLE A DEUX TETES et L'ETERNEL RETOUR: 1949. Scénario. Présentation par Lo Duca. Paris-Théâtre, Paris.

LES PARENTS TERRIBLES: 1949. Scénario. Présentation par Lo Duca. Le Monde Illustré théâtral et littéraire, no. 17, 11 décembre. Paris.

ORPHEE: 1949. Film. Scénario, dialogues et réalisation de J. Cocteau.

LES ENFANTS TERRIBLES: 1950. Scénario, réalisation, dialogues de J. Cocteau.

ORPHEE: 1951. Scénario. Illustré de photographies et d'un dessin de J. Cocteau. Editions Bonne, Paris.

LE SANG D'UN POETE: 1953. Scénario. Illustré de 50 photos de S. Masour. Editions du Rocher, Monaco.

VII. DISQUES

UN AMI DORT; BACCHUS (SCENES); AVEC L'AUTEUR. Philips. (Serge Reggiani; Jean-Louis Barrault et Jean Dessailly; Jean Cocteau).

TROIS POEMES (Les mauvais élèves—Le modèle des dormeurs—Le camarade) LE THEATRE DE JEAN COCTEAU. Columbia. (J. Cocteau).

LE FILS DE L'AIR—TIRADE DU SPHINX (de la Machine Infernale). Ultraphone. (J. Cocteau).

LES VOLEURS D'ENFANTS—LA TOISON D'OR. Columbia. (J. Cocteau).

TROIS POEMES (Le pigeon terreur—A l'encre bleue—Martingale)—TROIS POEMES (Le buste—Le théâtre grec —No man's land). Columbia (J. Cocteau).

ANNA LA BONNE. Columbia (Marianne Oswald).

LA VOIX HUMAINE. Columbia (Berthe Bovy).

LA DAME DE MONTE CARLO. Columbia (Marianne Oswald).

LE BEL INDIFFERENT. Columbia (Edith Piaf).

OEDIPUS REX (Stravinsky). Columbia (Stravinsky, Cocteau).

COMPLETE WORKS:

EDITIONS MARGUERAT, LAUSANNE

Vol. I.	1946	Le Grand Ecart. Thomas l'Imposteur. Les Enfants Terribles. Le Fantôme de Marseille.
Vol. II.	1947	Le Potomak (1913—14) Précédé d'un Prospectus (1916) et suivi de La Fin du Potomak (1939) Texte définitif.
Vol. III.	1947	Le Cap de Bonne Espérance. Poésies. Vocabulaire. Plaint-Chant. Cri Ecrit. Neiges.
	1947	Discours du Grand Sommeil. Opéra. Enigme. Allégories. Le Fils de l'Air. Léone. La Crucifixion.
Vol. V.	1948	Orphée. Oedipe Roi. Antigone. La Machine Infernale.
Vol. VI.	1948	Roméo et Juliette. Les Chevaliers de la Table Ronde. Renaud et Armide.
Vol. VII.	1948	Les Mariés de la Tour Eiffel. La Voix Humaine. Les Parents Terribles. Parade. Le Boeuf sur le Toit.

Vol. VIII.	1949	La Machine à Ecrire. Les Monstres Sacres. L'Ecole des Veuves. Le Bel Indifférent. Anna la Bonne. La Dame de Monte Carlo. Le Fantôme de Marseille.
Vol. IX.	1950	Le Rappel à l'Ordre. Le numéro Barbette. Lettre à Jacques Maritain. La Jeunesse et le Scandale. Une entrevue sur la critique avec Maurice Rouzaud. Rousseau.
Vol. X.	1950	Le Mystère laïc. Opium. Des beaux-arts considérés comme un assassinat. Quelques articles. Préfaces. Le Mythe du Gréco. Coupures de presse.

TRANSLATIONS AND ADAPTATIONS INTO ENGLISH OF WORKS BY JEAN COCTEAU

Novels

The Grand Ecart. Translated by Lewis Galantière. G. P. Putnam's Sons. New York, London, 1925. Retranslated as *The Big Mistake* (translation by Dorothy Williams). Peter Owen, London 1958.

Thomas the Impostor. Translated by Lewis Galantière. D. Appleton & Co., New York, London 1925. Retranslated as *The Impostor* (translation by Dorothy Williams). Peter Owen, London 1957.

Enfants Terribles. Translated by Samuel Putnam. Harcourt Brace & Co., New York, 1930. Retranslated as *Children of the Game* (translation by Rosamond Lehmann). Harvill Press, London, 1955. New Directions, New York, 1956.

Plays

Antigone. Translated by Carl Wildman. (Unpublished).

Orphée. Translated by Carl Wildman. Oxford University Press. London, 1933.

The Human Voice. Translated by Carl Wildman. Vision Press. London, 1951.

The Infernal Machine. Translated by Carl Wildman. Oxford University Press. London, 1936. In *International Modern Plays,* in Everyman's Library, E. P. Dutton & Co., New York. 1950. (Revised).

The Knights of the Round Table. Translated by W. H. Auden. (Unpublished).

Intimate Relations (Les Parents Terribles). Translated by Charles Frank. (Unpublished).

The Typewriter. Translated by Ronald Duncan. Dennis Dobson, London, 1948.

The Holy Terrors (Les Monstres Sacrés). Translated by Edward Owen Marsh. (Unpublished).

The Eagle has Two Heads. Adapted by Ronald Duncan. Vision Press, London 1948. Funk & Wagnalls Co., New York, 1948.

Bacchus. Mary C. Hoeck (Unpublished).

GENERAL WORK

Cock and Harlequin. Notes concerning music. Translated by Rollo H. Myers. With a portrait of the author and two monograms by Pablo Picasso. Egoist Press. London, 1921.

A Call to Order. Written between the years 1918 and 1926 and including *Cock and Harlequin, Professional Secrets* and other critical ~~...~~ Faber & Gwyer. London, 1926.

Opium. The diary of an Addict. Translated by Ernest Boyd. Longmans, Green & Co., London and New York, 1932. Reissued in 1933 by Allen & Unwin, London. Retranslated by Margaret Crosland and Sinclair Road. Peter Owen, London, 1957.

Round the World Again in Eighty Days (Mon Premier Voyage). Translated by Stuart Gilbert. Routledge. London, 1937. Retranslated as *Journey Round the World* (translation by W. J. Strachan). Peter Owen, London, 1958.

The Diary of a Film (La Belle et la Bête. Journal d'un Film). Translated by Ronald Duncan. Dennis Dobson Ltd., 1950.

Cocteau on the Film (Entretiens autor du Cinématographe). Translated by Vera Traill. Dennis Dobson Ltd., 1954.

Paris Album 1900—1914 (Portraits-Souvenir). Translated by Margaret Crosland. W. H. Allen, London, 1956.

Maalesh. Translated by Mary C. Hoeck. Peter Owen, London, 1956.

Hand of a Stranger (Journal d'un Inconnu). Translated by Alec Brown. Elek Books, London 1956.